Legal and Criminal Justice System under the Cooch Behar Raj

(1863–1911)

Legal and Criminal Justice System under the Cooch Behar Raj

(1863–1911)

Joydeep Pal

ABHIJEET PUBLICATIONS
NEW DELHI 110002

ABHIJEET PUBLICATIONS
4658-A, First Floor, Ambika Bhawan,
21 Ansari Road, New Delhi 110002
Phone: 011-23259444
E-mail: abhijeetpublication@gmail.com
www.abhijeetpublications.com

LEGAL AND CRIMINAL JUSTICE SYSTEM UNDER THE COOCH BEHAR RAJ (1864-1911)

First Published 2020

ISBN 978-93-88865-41-8

PRINTED IN INDIA

Published by J.K. Singh for Abhijeet Publications, New Delhi-110002, Lasertypeset by Abhijeet Typesetters, New Delhi and Printed at Dynamic Printers, New Delhi.

In
memory
of
my grandfather
Late Sudhir Chandra De Sarkar
Former I.P.S. Officer

Preface

Indian Administration from Ancient to Modern times was a part and parcel of Ideological Historiography. In the way of Ideological historiography world history glorifies the different aspects of various castes, races. In this connection the History of Indian Historiography visualizes an important aspect which is known as history of modernisation. Here when we call modernisation we mean two things. First of all modern outlook of the ongoing system and secondly the borrower who gave it a new term character and meaning. During the Colonial Period regional history more or less a period of monarchical regime of the social structure. During the particular period Princely State like Cooch Behar visualize the political correspondence in between Princely State and the mighty British Raj which has been categorised as a remarkable feature in the regional history of Bengal. Such a relation gave the birth of a well framed administrative structure in the monarchical State during the Colonial Period.

Modern Indian Historical period more or less connected with the history of freedom struggle of Indians against the Colonial Masters and during the so called period some important political issues evolved in the history of Cooch Behar, the tiny princely State in North–East frontier of India. The concept of political issues is not an exception to that. Indian regional historical period during Colonial regime witnessed a distinct landmark which is known as period of Colonial custody, which reflects an unforgettable scenario in Colonial India. Their works, determination and contribution has been scattered ly found in different books. An attempt has been made in the present context to sum up the day to day administrative measures of the State under Maharaja Nripendra Narayan (1863–1911), known as the harbinger of modernisation in the State of Cooch Behar.

In this connection few lines must be conclude, which motivate me to work on the concept of history of administrative theme. During the period 2004–2015 I have spent time (physically and by phone) with my academic mentors, Late Professor Jasobanta Kar (Professor of the Department of History, University of North Bengal), Professor Chhanda Chakraborty (Professor of Department of History, University of North Bengal). These academic gentlemen's guided me, how to study on the concept of administrative modernisation and also of classical political correspondence. The present study is a summary of the conversation cum lectures and academic guidance of Professor Kar and Professor Chakroborty. In this connection it is to be noted that administrative and political issues are the two sides of a same coin. Without administrative reformation a modern state cannot claim its modern (out and out modern). I have no hesitation to say that the above-mentioned academicians also guided me how to write on this very topic. I am the luckiest person, get the opportunity to discuss my theme with these eminent Professors. Although some other notable academicians also inspired me with their inspirations, suggestions and skills in this academic venture (as mentioned in the acknowledgements part of the work).

Joydeep Pal

Acknowledgements

The difficult task, for a researcher, is to acknowledge his indebtedness to all of them who took part in one way or the other, in shaping his thought – process and ideas, rather difficult to mention all of them by name. However, it is imperative to express my gratitude to them who are directly and indirectly associated with this study.

First of all, I must express a deep sense of gratitude to Late Professor Jasobanta Kar, for his eminently, scholarly, meticulous and inspiring guidance – a constant source of inspiration and encouragement and progress of this work.

I am also indebted to Professor Chhanda Chakraborty (former), Department of History, University of North Bengal, encouraged me by valuable suggestions and relevant sources from her own collections.

I also recall Professor Ratna Roy (Sanyal), {(former) Department of History, University of North Bengal}, Dr. Nilangshu Sekhar Das, Principal, Sukanta Mahavidyalaya, Professor Suresh Jnaneswaran, Dean of faculty of Social Sciences, University of Kerala, showed their interest for this work by rendering few rare sources connected with this work. It was really a rare opportunity for me to develop my idea with a comparative view and knowledge about this work.

I am benefited from Prof. I. Sarkar (former, Department of History, University of North Bengal), suggestions, academic skills, mentorship patience and encouragement for my study.

My heartfelt thanks to Professor Nirban Basu, (former, Department of History, University of Calcutta) have ever shown his interest and extended academic help whatever possible for him.

Thanks are due to my childhood friends, Colleagues for their constant help, inspiration and mental support in this academic venture.

Sources have not always been easy to find, but my labours have been eased by the courtesy of the staff of the following libraries: National Library (Kolkata), West Bengal State Archives (Kolkata), National Archives (New Delhi), Nehru Memorial Museum and Library (New Delhi), North Bengal State Library (Cooch Behar), University of North Bengal's Library.

Needless to mention, no words will be adequate to express my gratitude to the members of my family who have stood by me over these long testing times in the accomplishment of my study.

Joydeep Pal

Contents

Introduction

Before we going to discuss on the proposed theme, a general outline on the Princely State of Cooch Behar need to mention in the initial part of the work. The name Cooch Behar is a compound of two words, viz, Cooch and Behar.[1] The term Cooch is a corrupted form of Coch, or Koch being the name of a race of people inhabiting a large tract of North-East part of Bengal, north–east is more less one of the important section of the political discussion since ancient times.[2] Behar on the other hand more popularly known as Vihara donetes abode or sport. So in general way it exposes that Cooch Behar means the abode or land of the Koches. In the second sense, the compound means the land of sporting or dalliance with the Koches and has a mythological allusion to the vihar of god Mahadeva with the Koch damsels. In fact the same god is described in mythology to be the progenitor of the present line of the rulers of Cooch Behar.[3] The second interpretation of the term, however, ultimately leads to the first and the proper sense of the name Cooch Behar, therefore, is in either case, the land of the Koches. The significance of the word Cooch Behar points to a larger extent of country than the present small State of Cooch Behar for the Koch people is not confined to this State but is found in the neighbouring British Districts as well. The fact is, the territorial extent of Cooch Behar was at one time much larger than what it is now. As at present limited, Cooch Behar is a Feudatory State in Bengal in political relations with the British Government.[4]

Geographically, the state of Cooch Behar forms part of the Lower Provinces of Bengal and occupies a place in their north–east corner. It is about 20 miles south of the Bhutan ranges of the Himalayas, the tract of the country lying between the fool of the hills, and its northern frontier being the Western Duars which now form the eastern part of the District of Jalpaiguri. The Brahmaputra, just as it turns south from its westerly course, a short way below Dhubri, is at about the same distance from its eastern borders. It lies between 25 degree 57 ft. 40 inch and 26 degree 32 feet 20 inches, north latitude and between 88 degree 47 feet 40 inches and 89 degree 54 feet 35 inches east longitude.[5]

Cooch Behar is bounded on the north by the Western Duars which form the eastern part of the District of Jalpaiguri; on the east by the Guma Duars and Parganas Gaibari and Bhitarband of Rungpore, the rivers Gadadhar, Sankosh, Bagmi and Mara Dudkumar nearly forming the boundary line for a considerable distance; on the South by Chakla Purvabhag and Parganas Kakina and Kazirhat in the district of Rungpore and Pargana Patgram in the District of Jalpaiguri and on the west by Pargana Kazirhat in Rungpore and Chakla Boda in Jalpaiguri. With the exception of a few miles of the rivers Jaldhaka and kaljani in the north, the Gadadhar and the Sankosh in the east and the Dhaarla in the South the boundary is artificial on every side and prevents isolation of the South form the surrounding British territory.[6]

Apart from that here it can be said that the history of Cooch Behar represents around 450 years of historical analysis. The kingdom was started its journey with its well known ruler Maharaja Nara Narayan (1554 – 1587 AD), although the dynasty begin its journey with Maharaja Vishwa Sinha in 1522 AD. During his reign the kingdom of Cooch Behar was an extensive kingdom and comprised, in addition to the little State of Cooch Behar of the present day, almost the whole of North Bengal, Bhutan, Assam etc., as well as the modern State of Kachhar, Jaintia, Manipur, Tripura and extended up to the coast of the Bay of Bengal. Nara Narayan was decidedly the more powerful of the kings of the large extent of the Country which once formed the ancient kingdom of Kamrupa.[7] He along with his brother Shukladhwaja popularly known as Chila Roy formed an extremely efficient powerful role as a king. After him a number of rulers like Laxmi Narayan (1587 – 1621), Bira Narayan (1621–25), Prana Narayan (1625-1665), Moda Narayan (1665–80), Vasu Dev Narayan (1680–82), Mahendra Narayan (1682–1693), Rupa Narayan (1693–1714), Upendra Narayan (1714–1763), Devendra Narayan (1763-1765) ascended the throne, but due to political turmoil could not capitalize on the power. After them during the reign of Maharaja Dhairyendra Narayan (1765–1783) the State of Cooch Behar saw the shadow of misfortune in each and every sphere. In order to cope with the prevailing condition of the State Maharaja asked the British to help him, and as usual the Colonial powers took the advantage of the situation and extended their military help towards Maharaja. Accordingly in 1773 an agreement has been made in between the two which was as follows:[8]

- That the said Raja will immediately pay into the hands of the Collector of Rungpore Rs. 50,000 to defray the expenses of the force sent to assist him.
- That is more than Rs. 50,000 are expended the Raja make it good to the Honorable the English East India Company, but in case any part of it remains unexpended that it be delivered back.
- That the Raja will acknowledge subjection to the will of the English East India Company upon his country being cleared of his enemies and will allow the Cooch Behar to be annexed to the Province of Bengal.
- That the Raja further agrees to make over to the English India Company one-half of the annual revenues of Cooch Behar for ever.

- That the other money shall remain to the Raja and his heirs for ever, provided he is firm in his allegiance to the Honorable United East India Company.
- That in order to ascertain the value of the Cooch Behar State, the Raja will deliver a 'hastabud' (revenue statement) of his district into the hands of such person as the Honorable the President and Council of Calcutta shall think proper to depute for that purpose, upon, which valuation the annual malguzari (assessment) which the Raja is to pay, shall be established.
- That the amount of malguzari settled by such person as the Honorable East India Company shall depute, shall be perpetual.
- That the Honorable East India Company shall always assist the Raja with a force when he has occasion for it, for the defense of the country, the Raja bearing the expenses.
- That this treaty shall remain in force for the space of two years or till such time as advice may be received from the Court of Directors empowering the President and Council to ratify the same for ever.

The treaty signed and sealed and concluded by the Honorable the President and Council at Fort William, the fifth day of April 1773, on the one part and by Dharendra Narayan Raja of Cooch Behar at Behar Fort, the 6th Magh 1179, Bengal style, on the other part.

After the conclusion of the Treaty a small force, consisting of four companies of sepoys and two field-guns under the Command of Captain Jones, came up to the town of Cooch Behar. The force took the town by storm and not only drove back the Bhutias beyond the frontier but followed them up across the Duars and entering the hills, captured the forests of Pussakha and Dalimkota as well as the stockade of Chichakhata at which latter place a somewhat determined resistance was made by the Bhutias.[9]

It is true that after the conclusion of the treaty the king returned to the State and resumed the government of the State, he was in a melancholy state of mind and never afterwards showed any disposition to take any share in the management of the affairs of the State. As mentioned earlier Cooch Behar became a feudatory State by virtue of the Treaty of 1773 and Maharaja Dhairyendra Narayan, on whose behalf the treaty was concluded by the Nazir Deo who acknowledged his allegiance to the British Government. Although the next ruler of the State Maharaja Harendra Narayan (1783-1839) ascended the thrown at the age of 3 years 9 months. His period can be said as the rule of the last independent king, under whose guidance the State saw the vision of a monarchical reign free from any kind of foreign domination. The English Company since 1773 each and every aspect tried to involve in the internal affairs of the State of Cooch Behar, but due to independent attitude of Maharaja Harendra Narayan they could not fulfill their desired dream. After the death of Maharaja Harendra Narayan East India Company had the free run in the State and the son of Maharaja Harendra Narayan, Maharaja Shivendra Narayan (1839–47) who had friendly relations with the British, had their automatic choice in the State. During his rule in 1840, a Court of Justice for the final jurisdiction of civil, revenue and criminal cases was established and Dewan Kali Chandra Lahiri and Isanchandra Mustafi were made judges of the Court. From that period Maharaja used to sit in this Court to hear difficult cases, which he decided with the assistance of the above mentioned officers and learned persons.[10] In 1841 he formed Dharma Sabha in order to decide the dispute in internal administrations. Such kind of initiatives shows that the process of jurisprudence got the initial momentum under his rule.[11] After him under the rule of Maharaja Narendra Narayan (1847-1863) kingdom shows some sort of advanced reforms in administration. In 1848, the territory of Cooch Behar as long as it might be managed or superintended in its management, was placed under the jurisdiction of Government of Bengal, all question, however, of an important political bearing being referred to the Supreme Government. His shorter period of rule ushered an era of modern outlook in the State with the helping hand of the

British. Here it can be mentioned that the British Government in the matter of Cooch Behar State took friendly measures most probably because of its geographical local, represent the tiny State in the north–east frontier part of India which was vulnerable since ancient period as mentioned earlier.[12] The foundation of British Paramountcy in Western India was the network of treaties and engagements concluded with the Princely States between 1730 to 1881. The earliest dated 1730 and 1773 dealt with the suppression of piracy. In course of time it has been noticed that only the larger States became associated with the British directly via the medium of treaties. The rest were brought in almost accidentally by virtue of their diplomatic or feudal ties with the 'country' powers. British Officers like William Lee-Warner has called the feudatory policy of the East India Company a policy of 'subordinate isolation' —— a phrase first coined at the time of Lord Hastings.[13] It was 'sub–ordinate' because of the government's insistence on the states relinquishing the right to conduct their own foreign relations; it was one of 'isolation' because, with the conspicuous exceptions of the states that were annexed and to a lesser extent, the Company was content to leave the darbars very much to their own devices.[14]

During the 1820s and 1830s, British residents and political agents were appointed to the more important native courts; and to the extent that these men were on the spot they were able to keep the government reasonably well-informed about what was going on in the territories under princely rule. But except in the matter of infanticide, the Company made no attempt to act on the information received. To the extent that a commitment to mission civilisation was beginning to gain strength in British India, there was as yet little evidence of its influence in the realm of feudatory policy.[15]

One of the central arguments running through this work is that the similarities in the patterns of indirect rule appear from analysis of local practice of this form of imperialism in the context of official policy by the imperial government, rather than either practice or policy alone.

'Indirect rule' as an explicit term was not current before the twentieth century, even in India, where the practice developed.[16] There, officials used a variety of labels for the practice of indirect rule including British 'Paramountcy' or 'Suzerainty' or 'Native Administration' over 'Princely', 'Protected', 'Native States'. Much more consistently, however, other imperial administrations ——— following the British pattern established in India ——— have commonly used the 'Resident' to designate their agent of indirect rule. This continuity suggests that the pattern of indirect rule developed by the British in India served as the model in these later colonial governments.[17]

During the Twentieth Century, European and non–European writers about imperialism have tried to make 'indirect rule' a precise technical term. Yet they have tried to apply 'indirect rule' to a broad variety of practices, drawn from a vast geographical and chronological range. As a result, debate has raged over whether particular historical examples fit one or another definition of indirect rule. In this connection it can be stated that trying to induce a definition from imperial practice, some writers have fitted an extremely narrow definition on the term others have applied it so freely that it becomes only a vogue concept.[18] More or less indirect rule helped State like Cooch Behar to modernize itself under advanced modern ruler. During the rule of Maharaja Nripendra Narayan (1863–1911) new initiatives has been introduced in every sphere of Cooch Behar State, which can be categorised as a mode of influence of indirect rule. The ruler unconsciously, sub-consciously, and consciously delivered the good things for the welfare of the State.[19] According to official records the need of regular organized system of Police was one of the major issue of the State authority which form the backbone of the administration, it can be compared with the administration of land settlement which was one the major issue of the State, and the authority well known that the issue need to be solved as early as possible.[20] Ever since the State came into contact with the English, one of the earliest endeavors of Government had been to organize an efficient system of administration in the State.

NOTES AND REFERENCES

1. Chowdhuri. H.N, *The Cooch Behar State and its Land Revenue Settlement*, Cooch Behar State Press, Cooch Behar, 1903, p. 2.
2. *Ibid*.
3. *Ibid*., p. 3.
4. *Ibid*., p. 250.
5. *Ibid*.
6. *Ibid*.
7. *Ibid*.
8. *Ibid*., p. 254.
9. *Ibid*.
10. *Ibid*.
11. *Ibid*., p. 276.
12. *Ibid*., p. 277.
13. Copland, Ian, *The British Raj and The Indian Princes Paramountcy in Western India (1857 – 1930)*, Orient Longman, Bombay, 1987, p. 43.
14. *Ibid*.
15. *Ibid*.
16. Fisher, Michael H., *Indirect Rule in India – Residents and the Residency System (1764-1858)*, Oxford University Press, 1991, p. 4.
17. *Loc.cit*.
18. *Ibid*., p. 5.
19. Chowdhuri. H.N, *op.cit*., p. 269.
20. *Ibid*.

1

Department of Civil Justice in Cooch Behar State

The administration of Civil justice in the State of Cooch Behar was in a systematic way carryon its day to day work during the monarchical Period. Here it need to mention that during the rule of Maharaja Nripendra Narayan specially from 1878 (when he attained maturity) the State of Cooch Behar got a momentum. A brief summary on the said theme may be discussed in the following way:

In 1878–79 the number of regular suits instituted was 3,810 against, 3,143 of the preceding year, showing an increase of 667 cases. Such kind of increase was due to the fact that the term of grace in extension of the period of limitation under the new Act was to expire on the 31st March 1879 and the further extension, granted was not sanctioned until just before the close of the year.[1] A number of suits were therefore instituted in pursuance of old claims to save limitation. The further period of grace was sanctioned in consideration of the hardness of the times, and of the fact that a number of jotedars and mahajanas had petitioned for it. Six months only were ranted; the Act therefore comes into full operation of the 1st October 1879. There is no doubt that to refuse the further extension of the period of grace would have forced claims into court which may yet be amicably adjusted and would have brought ruin to many and probably interfered in no small degree with the collection of the State revenue.[2]

The number of regular suits disposed of during the year was 3,477 against 3,125 of the previous year. Although there were thus more cases decided, the disposals did not keep pace with the institutions and at the close of the year the large number of 576 cases remained pending.[3] But the institutions were not equally distributed over the year, a large number of plants being filed towards the close of the year, for reasons given above. Some efforts was made by the presiding officers to keep their files down, but I think more might have been done. A circular addressed to all officers with Civil jurisdiction during the last quarter of the year had the effects of bringing down the files considerably, but the number of cases pending over six months untill unduly large on some files.[4]

The health of the Dewani Ahilkar has been failing lately. He took priviledge leave for two months at the time of the Durja Puja holidays. During his absence the Fauzdari Ahilkar carried on the duties of his office, but was unable to devote his whole time to it and consequently the file fell the arrears.[5] After his return from privilege leave, he again fell ill and had to take sick leave. It was then arranged that another officer should officiate for him and the work did not suffer, but the state of the officers health prior to his going on leave was prejudicial to his efficiency and his file showed an undue number of pending cases. He has again rejoined his office, but has been advised and intends to retire on pension, as he is an old man and by constitutional infirmities unfitted for hard sedentary work.[6]

The number, nature and value of suits instituted and disposed of by all courts during 1877-78 and 1878 -79 are shown in the three sub-joined tables:[7]

Out of the 1,739 cases instituted and re-admitted in the Dewani Ahilkar's Court during the past year 817 cases were transferred to the Assistant's Court, for trial.

The number of Miscellaneous cases disposed of during the year was 453 against 431 of the previous year. The following table shows the number of suits disposed of by

	INSTITUTED		DISPOSED OF		PENDING	
	1877 -78	1878 - 79	1877 -78	1878 - 79	1877 - 78	1878- 79
	3,143	3,810	3,125	3,477	245	576
Increase	-------	667	-----	352	-----	331
Decrease	-------	----	-----	-----	-----	-----

Description of Suits	Number in 1877-78	Number in 1878 - 79	Value in 1877 - 78	Value in 1878 - 79
			Rs. A. P.	Rs. A. P.
Suits of Small Cause Court Class	2,726	3,277	1,35,176 4 8	4,69,249 13 9
Other Suits -----------------	417	533	1,88,355 8 7	1,62,749 0 4
Total -------	3,148	3,810	3,23,531 13 3	3,31,998 14 1
Increase ---------------------	---------	667	----------------	8,467 0 10
Decrease ---------------------	--------	-----	----------------- -	------------

Class of Courts	Instituted and Re-admitted		Disposed Of.		Pending	
	1877 -78	1878 -79	1877-78	1878 -79	1877-78	1878 -79
Dewani Ahilkar	1600	1739	880	855	89	187
Assistant to ditto	33	47	695	774	73	158
Dinhata sub-divisional Court	511	627	537	586	55	93
Mathabhanga	650	918	645	780	21	134
Mekhligunj	349	479	368	482	7	4
Total	3,143	3,810	3,125	3,477	245	576

each of the Courts during during the year and the number pending at the end:[8]

CLASS OF COURTS	Disposed of		Pending	
	1877 - 78	1878 – 79	1877 – 78	1878 – 79
Dewani Ahilkar	227	209	56	89
Court -------------	43	77	26	14
Assistant's Court -----------------	58	40	5	27
Dinhata Sub –divisional Court ---	43	60	5	18
Mathabhanga --------------------	00	67	------	3
---	481	453	92	151
Mekhligunj -----------------------	------	22	-------	59
-	------	------	------	-------
TOTAL -------------------------				
-				
Increase -----------------------				
-				
Decrease -----------------------				
-				

decisions in original suits disposed of and pending as compared with the preceeding year:[10]

Class of Courts	Completely	Partially	Amount realized
Dewani Ahilkar	305	562	34,112 3 3
Assistanat to Ahilkar	125	127	4,335 9 9
Naib, Ahilkar, Dinhata	60	117	1,324 11 7
Ditto , Mathabhanga	112	167	8,946 15 10
Ditto, Mekhligunj	105	158	8,749 7 10
Total	707	1,131	57,469 0 3

	Instituted		Disposed of				Pending			
	1877-78	1878-79	1877-78		1878-79		1877 - 78		1878 – 79	
	In Judges and Dewani Ahilkar's Court	In Judges and Dewani Ahilkar's Court	Judge	Dewani Ahilkar	Judge	Dewani Ahilkar	Judge	Dewani Ahilkar	Judge	Dewani Ahilkar
Increase	133	173	67	57	80	74	55	12	56	30
Decrease	-----	40	-----	----	13	17	----	----	1	18
	------	-----	-----	----	-----	----	----	-----	----	----

Appeals Form	No. of cases tried	Pending from last year	No. of appeals preferred	TOTAL	No. of decisions affirmed	No. reversed or modified	Otherwise disposed of	Pending
Babu RamChandra Ghosh Dewani ahilkar	1,064	36	52	88	34	10	9	35
Kumar Rangila Narayan	549	12	22	34	13	6	11	04
Assist. And Naib Ahilkar	851	3	23	26	7	6	13	-------
Mekhligunj	------	-------	27	27	6	1	3	17
Babu Payari Lall Roy, Assit. And Naib Ahilkar Dinhata	626	8	33	41	11	1	11	18
Babu hari Das Mukherjee, Offg. Ditto	840	9	16	25	6	4	3	12
BabuSashi Bhusan Halder, Naib ahilkar, Dinhata and Mathabhanga								
Babu Kedar Nath Mukherjee, Naib ahilkar, Mathabhanga and Mekhligunj								

Appeals Form	No. of cases tried	Pending from last year	No. of appeals preferred	TOTAL	No. of decisions affirmed	No. reversed or modified	Otherwise disposed of	Pending
Babu RamChandra Ghosh	200	9	10	19	3	1	5	10
Dewani ahilkar								
Kumar Rangila Narayan	67	1	4	5	-------	------	1	1
Assist. And Naib Ahilkar	77	-----	4	4	1	------	3	-------
Mekhliganj	------	-------	1	1	1	-------	1	-------
Babu Payari Lall Roy, Assit. And Naib Ahilkar Dinhata	40	1	3	4	------	-------	1	3
Babu hari Das Mukherjee, Offg. Ditto	60	1	------	1	-------	--------	1	-------
BabuSashi Bhusan Halder, Naib ahilkar, Dinhata and Mathabhanga								
Babu Kedar Nath Mukherjee, Naib ahilkar, Mathabhanga and Mekhliganj								

apprentiees to High Court pleaders for three consecutive years after obtaining their certificate of B.L., unless employed in work of a judicial nature under Government should they fail to do, they forfiet all benefit from their degree.[13]

The effect of this order is to close the doors of our Courts, contrary to our desire, to young Bachelors of Law and to throw us on our own resources as regards a supply of competent pleaders for the Higher Courts. This is much to be regretted. A few educated pleader with a knowledge of English are a great desideratum here, as apart from the value of their assistance to the Deputy Commissioner in his capacity of judge, they form a reserve on which to draw for competent men to fill up officiating appointments both judicial and executive.[14]

The High Court may be induced to make an exception in our favour and to allow service in Cooch Behar whether on the bench or at the bar to count as time passed in practice or in Government service under the Bengal Government.

During the year 1880-81, the number of regular suits instituted under report was 2,284 against 7,639 of the preceding year. There was a decrease of 5,355 cases and this decrease was due to the operation of the Limitation Act in 1879 – 80, on which account an unusually large number of suits were instituted in that year. Earlier records has fully explained the abnormal influx of litigation in 1879–80 and the somewhat exceptionally low figures of the year under review may be accounted for by the excessive litigation of the previous year on the principle that after the storm comes the calm. The number of regular suits dis[posed of during the year was 3,301 against 6,549 of the previous year.[15]

Table I and II will show the number, nature and value of suits instituted and disposed of by all the Courts during 1879-80 and 1880–81. They will also show the number of cases pending at the close of the year. The table III will show the number of cases instituted and disposed of by each of the courts during the year and the number pending at the end.[16]

Table showing suits instituted, disposed of and pending in the past year as compared with the preceding year:[17]

No. I

	Instituted		*Disposed of*		*Pending*	
	1879–80	*1880–81*	*1879–80*	*1880-81*	*1879–80*	*1880–81*
Decrease	7639	2284	6549	3301	1666	649
	———	5355	———	3248	———	1017

No. II

Description of suits	Number in 1879-80	Number in 1880-81	Value in 1879-80	Value in 1880-81
			Rs. A. P.	Rs. A. P.
Suits of Small Cause Court Class	7, 067	1,977	3,91,695 8 0	98,686 7 2
Other suits	572	307	1,51,465 8 7	97,940 9 8
Total -----------------------	7,639	2,281	5,43,161 0 7	196627 0 10
	-------	5,355	--------------	346533 15 9

No. III

Class of courts	Instituted and readmitted		Disposed of		Pending	
	1879-80	1880-81	1879-80	1880-81	1879-80	1880-81
Naib Ahilkar	5,475	1007	1,895	691	179	106
Assistant Ahilkar	30	36	1,081	494	199	142
Additional Naib Ahilkar	3	15	314	236	205	49
Dinhata ditto	1,530	373	1,053	774	570	167
Mathabhanga ditto	1,675	541	1,416	779	383	143
Mekhligunj ditto	916	312	790	397	130	42
Total	7,639	2,284	6,540	3,301	1,666	649

were respectively transferred to the Assistant's and the additional Naib Ahilkar's courts.

Table showing miscellaneous cases of a Judicial nature other than regular suits or proceedings in execution, disposed of and pending in each of the Courts:[18]

No. IV

Class of courts	*Disposed of.*		*Pending*	
	1879 - 80	*1880 - 81*	*1879 - 80*	*1880 -81*
Dewani Ahilkar	236	246	102	113
Assistanat ditto	42	49	36	25
Additional Naib Ahilkar	10	41	17	14
Dinhata ditto ditto	59	94	52	64
Mathabhanga ditto	58	72	46	46
Mekhligunj do do	78	104	11	7
Total	483	606	264	269

Class of Courts	Completely	Partially	Amount realised		
			Rs.	A.	P.
Dewani Ahilkar	488	695	53,735	10	6
Assistant ditto	151	192	8,213	6	2
AdditionalNaibAhilkar	35	61	4,116	2	9
Dinhata ditto ditto	117	152	2,230	15	2
Mathabhangadittoditto	182	310	14,578	13	3
Mekhligunj ditto	119	213	10,631	6	5
TOTAL	1,092	1,623	23,506	6	3

Comparative table showing the number of appeals from the decisions in original suits disposed of and pending:[19]

	Instituted		Disposed of				Pending			
	1879-80	1880-81	1879 -80		1880 -81		1897-80		1880 - 81	
	In the judges and Dewani Ahilkars Court	In the judges and Dewani Ahilkars Court	Judge	Dewani Ahilkar	Judge	Dewani Ahilkar	Judge	Dewani Ahilkar	Judge	Dewani Ahilkar
	158	180	62	70	111	93	76	36	55	31
Increase	----	22	----	------	49	31	---	-----	-----	------
Decrease	-----	-----	- -----	------	--- -	------	----- -	------	21	5

Appeals from	No. of cases tried	Pending from last year	No. of appeals preferred	Total	No. of decisions affirmed	No. reversed or modified	Otherwise disposed of	Pending
Babu Ramchandra Ghosh, Naib Ahilkar	621	17	39	56	18	10	6	22
Babu Priya nath dutt, Offg, Dewani Ahilkar	---------	17	1	18	10	4	4	----
Babu Peary Lal Roy, Sudder Naib Ahilkar	384	40	46	86	12	47	16	11
Babu Hari Das Mukherjee, Additional Naib Ahilkar	110	2	38	40	11	2	4	23
Babu Rameshwar Pramanik, do do	282	----	15	15	4	1	4	6
Babu Sashi Bhusan Halder, naib Ahilkar, dinhata	675	11	29	29	5	3	11	10
Babu Kadar Nath mukherjee, Naib Ahilkar Mathabhanga, mekhligunj	596	8	23	23	8	4	4	7
Kumar Rangila Narayan, Naib Ahilkar Mekhligunj	397	15	24	24	6	3	8	7
Babu Bireshawar Palit, sub registrar	----	1	1	1	---------	-------	1	----
Total	3,065	111	181	292	74	74	58	86

Appeals from	No. of cases tried	Pending from last year	No. of appeals preferred	Total	No. of decisions affirmed	No. reversed or modified	Otherwise disposed of	Pending
Babu Ramchandra Ghosh, Naib Ahilkar	236	5	11	16	6	4	1	5
Babu Priya nath dutt, Offg, Dewani Ahilkar	---------	1	------	1	-----	1	-----	-----
Babu Peary Lal Roy, Sudder Naib Ahilkar	42	1	4	5	2	------	2	1
Babu Hari Das Mukherjee, Additional Naib Ahilkar	10	-----	5	5	------	--------	1	4
Babu Sashi Bhusan Halder, naib Ahilkar, dinhata	59	1	3	4	1	1	--------	2
Babu Kadar Nath mukherjee, Naib Ahilkar Mathabhanga, mekhligunj	58	2	1	3	-------	1	1	1
Kumar Rangila Narayan, Naib Ahilkar Mekhligunj	78	3	------	3	1	---------	2	------------
Babu Bireshawar Palit, sub registrar	-------	1	-------	1	-----	----------	1	--------
Total	483	14	24	38	10	7	8	13

No. VI

Instituted		Disposed of		Pending	
1879 - 80	1880 - 81	1879 - 80	1880 -81	1879 - 80	1880 - 81
72	85	69	87	33	29
Increase	13	-------	18	----------	4

No. VII

Instituted		Disposed of		Pending	
1879 - 80	1880 - 81	1879 - 80	1880 -81	1879 - 80	1880 - 81
3	5	1	6	3	2
Increase	2	-------	5	---------	-------
Decrease	-------	--------	--------	---------	1

from	*preferred*	*to decisions*	*decisions affirmed*	*cases to decided*
Babu Pearylal Roy	23	6 percent	6	18 percent
Haridas Mukherjee	21	7 percent	11	69 percent
Sashi Bhusan Halder	11	2 percent	2	20 percent
Kadarnath Mukherjee 63 percent		8	1 percent	5
Kumar rungila Narayan	7	2 percent	6	55 percent
Rameswar Pramanik	14	5 percent	6	75 percent

No. IX

Miscellaneous appeals from	*Appeals preferred*	*Ratio of appeals to decisions*	*Number of decisions affirmed*	*Ratio of affirmed cases to decided*
Babu Pearylal Roy	3	6 percent	2	67 percent
Haridas Mukherjee	2	4 percent	——	——

The two following tables show the receipts and disbursements of the Courts under the control of the Dewani Ahilkar for the past and preceding years:[25]

RECEIPTS

	Value of stamps presented in different Courts		Fees, fines and sale proceeds & c.		TOTAL	
	Rs.	A. P.	Rs.	A.	Rs.	A. P.
1879 – 80	66,761	8 0	P.		84,844	0 3
1880 - 81	30,720	8 0	18,082	8 3	43,430	13 3
			12,710	5 3		
Decrease	36,041	0 0	5,372	3 0	41,413	3 0

DISBURSEMENT

	Salaries of preceding officers		Cost of estyablishment and other charges		TOTAL	
	Rs.	A. P.	Rs.	A.	Rs.	A. P.
1879 – 80	8,663	2 4	P.		14,883	7 3
1880 - 81	13,608	10 2	6,220	5 4	25,268	14 8
			11,660	4 6		
Increase	4,945	7 10	5,439	15	10,385	7 0
Decrease	---------	----	2		--------	---- -
	---		---------	-----	---	
			---			

of by each of the courts during the year and the number pending at the end.[26]

Table showing suits instituted, disposed of and pending in the past year as compared with the preceding year :[27]

Table showing number and value of suits of different kinds commenced in all courts in the past year as compared with the preceding year:[28]

No.I

	INSTITUTED		DISPOSED		PENDING	
	1881 -82	1882 - 83	1881 -82	1882 - 83	1881 -82	1882 -83
	2,798	3,336	3,030	3,102	417	651
Increase	------	538	------	72	------	234
Decrease	------	------	------	------	------	-----

No.II

Description of suits	No. of suits in 1881-82	Number of suits in 1882-83	Value in 1881-82		Value in 1882-83	
			Rs.	A. P.	Rs.	A. P.
Suits of small Cause Court Class	2,429	2,925	1,28,728	12 7	1,48,330	2 8
Other suits	369	411	63,095	5 8	63,642	0 0
Total	2,798	3,336	1,91,824	2 3	2,11,972	2 8
Increase	———	538	....		20,148	0 5
Decrease	....	....	....		....	....

No.III

CLASS OF COURTS	Instituted and re-admitted		Disposed of		Pending	
	1881-82	1882-83	1881-82	1882-83	1881-82	1882-83
Dewani Ahilkar	1,244	1,383	744	(a)622	82	114
Assistant Ahilkar	25	15	438	350	92	114
Additional Naib Ahilkar	15	14	201	334	33	95
Dinhata Naib Ahilkar	558	753	603	643	117	224
Mathabhanga Naib Ahilkar	641	810	721	801	63	68
Mekhligunj Ahilkar	315	361	323	352	30	36
Total	2,798	3,336	3,030	3,102	417	651

were respectively transferred to the Assistant's and the Additional Naib Ahilkar's Court.[30]

The number of miscellaneous cases, disposed of during the year, was 25 against 609 of the preceding year. The following table shows the number of miscellaneous suits disposed of by each of the Courts during the year and the number pending at the end.

Table showing miscellaneous cases of judicial nature other than regular suits and proceedings in execution, disposed of and pending in each of the Court :[31]

No. IV

CLASS OF COURTS	Disposed of		Pending	
	1881 – 82	1882 – 83	1881 – 82	1882 – 83
Dewani Ahilkar	258	185	80	114
Assistant ditto	58	24	14	8
Additional Naib Ahilkar	23	18	4	22
Dinhata ditto ditto	120	69	40	34
Mathabhanga ditto	85	90	25	21
Mekhligunj ditto	65	39	5	5
Total	609	425	168	204

No.V

Class of Courts	Completely	Partially	Amount Realized		
			Rs.	A.	P.
Dewani Ahilkar	145	1,127	49,744	10	6
Assistant ditto	72	201	6,809	2	3
Additional Naib Ahilkar	38	97	4,696	3	3
Dinhata ditto	155	221	1,570	6	0
Mathabhanga ditto	149	367	12,734	13	7
Mekhligunj ditto	107	184	7,968	6	11
TOTAL	666	2,197	83,523	10	6

No.VI

	Instituted		Disposed of.				Pending			
	1881- 82	1882 -83	1881 82		1882 -83		1881- 82		1882 -83	
	In the judge & Dewani Ahilkar's Court	In the Judge's &C Dewani Ahilkar's Court	Judge	Dewani Ahilkar	Judge	Dewani Ahilkar	Judge	Dewani Ahilkar	Judge	Dewani Ahilkar
	207	192	96	109	48	110	63	26	88	35
Increase	-------	-------	------	------	-----	1	----	----	25	9
Decrease	------	-------	-------	------	48	------	----	-----	-----	---

No.VII

Year	Instituted	Disposed of		Remarks
	In the Judge's Dewani Ahilkar's Court	Judge	Dewani Ahilkar	
1877 -78	133	67	57	
1878 -79	173	80	74	
1879 -80	158	62	70	
1880 -81	180	111*	93	*Out of this 31 cases were decided by one decision
1881 -82	207	96	109	
1882- 83	192	48	110	

No.VIII

APPEALS FROM	No. of cases tried	Pendin g from last year	No. of appeals preferre d	TOTA L	No. of decision s affrimed	No. revers ed or modif ied	Other wise dispo sed of	Pen ding	Ratio of appeals to decisio ns	Ratio of affirmed to decided
Calica Das Dutt, Dewan Ahilkar	-------	5	-----	5	5	-----	------	---	-----	100
Ram Chander Ghosh , Dewani Ahilkar	630	30	41	71	12	9	4	46	5Percet	48
Priya Nath Dutt, offg. Dewani Ahilkar	------	3	------	3	1	1	1	----	-----	33
Peary lal Roy, Naib Ahilkar	-----	3	2	5	1	1	3	----	------	20
Hari Das Mukherjee, Dewani Ahilkar	801	13	36	49	14	2	11	22	4	51
Rameswar Pramanik, Naib	21	5	12	17	5	2	4	6	57	45
Ahilkar	----	4	3	7	3	1	1	2	------	60
Sashi Bhusan Halder, Naib Ahilkar	377	5	9	14	1	2	2	9	2	20
Kader Nath Mukherjee, naib Ahilkar	156	12	21	33	7	9	8	9	13	29
Sita Nath Banerjee, Temporary Naib Ahilkar	67	3	15	18	10	1	2	5	22	77
Jogendra Nath Sanyal,	-----	5	6	11	7	1	2	1	------	70
Temporary Naib Ahilkar	111	1	5	6	1	-----	3	2	4	25
Krishna Dhann Benerjee, Temporary Naib Ahilkar	352	-----	20	20	5	-----	3	12	5	31
Rabindra Lal Shome, Naib Ahilkar, Mekhligunj	587	------	22	22	------	------	13	9	3	-----
Girish Chandra Sikdar, Naib Ahilkar, Dinhata										
Total	3,102	89	192	281	72	29	57	123		

	1881 - 82	*1882 -83*	*1881 - 82*	*1882 - 83*	*1881 - 82*	*1882 - 83*
	95	116	98	104	23	35
Increase		21	——	6	——	12
Decrease	——		——	——	——	——

Table showing miscellaneous appeals instituted, disposed of and pending in the past year as compared with the preceding year :

No. X

	Instituted		*Disposed of.*		*Pending*	
	1881 - 82	*1882 -83*	*1881 - 82*	*1882 - 83*	*1881 - 82*	*1882 - 83*
	9	3	8	6	3	——
Increase		6	——	2	——	3
Decrease	——		——	——	——	——

The general increase of work of all kinds in sub-divisions has necessiated proposals for reliving the officers of the hard worked Sub-divisions of Dinhata and Mathbhanga of Civil Work, as has been elsewhere stated in this report.

The two following tables show the receipts and disbursements of the Courts under the control of the Dewani ahilkar for the past and previous years:[36]

RECEIPTS

	Value of stamps presented in several courts			Fees, fines and sale proceeds &c.			Total		
	Rs.	A.	P.	Rs.	A.	P.	Rs.	A.	P.
1881 – 82	28,754	0	0	10,817	7	0	39,571	7	0
1882 -83	32,986	8	0	14,673	12	0	47,660	4	0
Increase	----------------			--------------------			8,088	13	0
Decrease	----------------			--------------------			--------------------		

DISBURSEMENTS

	Salaries of presiding officers			Cost of establishment and other charges			Total		
	Rs.	A.	P.	Rs.	A.	P.	Rs.	A.	P.
1881 – 82	12,218	0	0	9,990	0	0	22,208	0	0
1882 -83	13,009	0	0	9,734	0	0	22,743	0	0
Increase	791	0	0	---------------------			8,088	535	0
Decrease	----------------			---------------------			---------------------		

on the following objects :[37]

- Cooch Behar Town Committee Act.
- Rules relating to attachment and sale of live –stock and moveable property in execution of decrease.
- Law of Limitation relating to easements.
- Rules relating to the attachment and sale of intestate property.
- Adoption of British Indian Willa Act and the Probate Act.
- Age of majority of parties under the Court of Wards.
- Law reaching to minors and the constitution of the Cooch Behar Ward.
- Amendment of the Stamp Act.
- Service of summonses and writs outside the jurisdiction of Court issuing them.
- Judicial powers of the Dewan.
- Adoption of Section 642 of Act XIV of 1882 Civil Procure Code.
- Period of limitation for the correction of Settlement Record.

In detailed manner the above mentioned objects (notable ones) may be summarised as follows :[38]

1) The Maharaja in Council was pleased to sanction the constitution of a Municipality for the town of Cooch Behar and appointed a Committee consisting of the Superintendent of the State as President, the Dewan and the Superintendent of works as mentioned and the Fouzdari

Ahilkar as Secretary. Towards the close of 1885 – 86 the Municipal Committee submitted a Bill to provide for the appointment of Town Committees in Towns and other places in the State and to better provision for the conservancy, improvement and watching the things and levying of taxes there on. The discussion on the provisions of this took place in three different meetings. During the year under report certain additions and alterations were ordered and the draft Bill prepared. It has been drawn out on the lines of Bengal Council Act. To suit the reuirements of the State certain modifications had been taken. The Provisions of the Act have for the present been extended only to Town of Cooch Behar. The Municipal Committee consists of one official and 3 non –official memnbers. The financial condition of the Committee capacity and all necessary details has been recorded in the report which has been submitted to Vice – chairman of the Cooch behar Town Committee.

2) Rules relating to attachment and sale of live stock and all moveable property in execution of decrees, has been maintained in the State was considered with hardship and venience. The Rules prevailing in the Acts had therefore modified.

3) There being no distinct law regulating the acquisition, maintenance and extinction of the right of estimates, difficulties were experianced by the Civil Courts of the State in deciding suits which involved the determination of that right. The Civil Judge therefore proposed the adoption of the last Chapter of the Indian Limitation Act (XV OF 1877). The Maharaja in Council admitted the necessity legislation in this matter. The whole subject however, under consideration. It is to be decided if it would be expedient to accept 20 years as the limit of prescription.

4) In regard to departmental heads have been called upon submit detailed reports on the measures. With regards to Maharaja in Council has, in fact, ordered (for the benefit of the public) the promulgation of the decisions arrived at during your minority by the authorities. The age of a

minor under the Court of Wards has been fixed at 21 years.

5) Under this head the Maharaja in Council after full deliberation decided that in future 21 years should be the age of attaining majority by minor subject to the control of the Court of Wards and that with regard to all other minors 18 years should be recognised as the term of minority. The Maharaja in Council also adopted the British Indian Act XL OF 1858 as the Law of Cooch Behar with such alterations as are rendered necessary by all local requirements.

6) The administration with regard to the judicial functions of the Dewan, appearing to us to be somewhat ambiguous, referred the point to Maharaja for an authoritative decision in view of possible misinterpretation and hence possible questioning of the validity of any judicial proceedings held by that officer. The Superintendant of the state was of the opinion that "the Dewan will not exercise judicial power", in tended to be read with and to have application merely following words viz, "appeals from the decisions of the subordinates in rent –suits lying to the Civil Court". Maharaja concurred in the view and thought that the framers of the memo of Administration did not intend to convey that the Dewan should not exercise any judicial function, because such exclusion, if absolute, would interfare with his sitting as a Judge in the council Court.

7) Act VIII of 1859 which was in force in this State, with regard to the protection of parties or witnesses from arrest in execution of decrees while going to and from Court in the interest of their cases or for giving evidence. This ommission has been supplied by Section 642 of the New Code. The Officers resolved upon adopting this Section in the State. However, the matter came into force on the recommendation of the Superintendent of the State known as final orders.

8) During the work of settlement operations, Commissioner Mr. F.R.Cockerell passed a rule to the effect that suits for contesting the correctness of settlement records

were to be instituted within 3 years from the date of the issue of ther Patta for the jote in which the land in dispute was situated. Since the passing of this rule in 1875 the State Courts held that it was to apply to all cases involving changes in settlement records. In deciding a special appeal in 1882 Commissioner Lord H. Ulick Browne held, however that the general provosion of the Limitation Act, allowing 12 years as the period within which the suits for declaration of right and title might be instituted, could not be altered by the special rule passed by Mr. Cockerell. Such kind of decision gave rise to a correspondence which considered during the year. The point for decision was as to whether the view always taken by the Courts should be disturbed even during the term of the present settlement ans the law on the point reconstructed. There was some divergence of opinion on the question and as it seemed difficult to arrive at a definite conclusion, agreed to allow the question to await the test of a case in the Council Court.

Regarding the judicial functions of the State in Council have been fully stated in the report, as the highest Court in the State having final jurisdiction over criminal, revenue and civil suits and proceedings, the Council have to discuss and pass final orders on many important points. In the absence of distinct enacments these orders have the force of law and serve as guides to the lower courts.The Superintendent of the State have therefore thought it proper to order the publication of all our decisions on important points in the official Gazette.[39]

a) During the last year i.e in 1885 there were 23 sittings on the judicial side, at 10 of which Maharaja presided one person.

b) The number of Criminal appeals from the Sessions Court which were for disposal during the year was 5 of which 2 remained pending at the close of the year.

c) There were 2 regular appeals preferred during the year against 9 in 1884 -85. The number decided was 4 and that remained pending was 7.

d) Six miscellaneous appeals were instituted during the year against 18 of the previous year, 15 remained pending.

e) Together with 45 cases pending from the previous year total number of special appeals for the disposal of the Council during the year was 56, of which 34 remained pending. Of 35 motions 25 were disposed of during the year.

f) Detailed statements shows the institutions, disposals and pending cases were hereto appended.

The total number of cases of all sorts boarded for the 23 sittings during the year was 153, of which disposed of 59. It has been finally defend an average of 2.6 cases in each sitting. Many contested cases came up for hearing. Of these cases more than 2 or 3 could not be finally heard in the same day. In some instances a single case occupied for 2 or 3 sittings. It also happened that had to postpone cases owing to pressure of urgent departmental business. The results therefore were not unsatisfactory.[40]

In connection with the above mentioned subject it can be stated that during the year, with the view to promote administrative efficiency, the Process Service Establishment was distributed and separate allotment of Naib Nazirs and peons made to the Civil, Revenue, Criminal Departments; the arrangements under which the Nazir, who was to be paid from the Revenue Budget, could supervise the Nizarat work in all the three Departments, were not however disturbed.[41] The process service establishment in the sub –divisions were not distributed. The State authority introduced certain additional rules for the sorting of Civil records and resolved upon having a record–room for the State Council, in which shall be kept all the records of the previous Rajshava, those of the Commissioners Office, the Settlement and Survey records and in fact all records which in the record room of the Superintendent of the State, excepting those which appertain to his Department and which in view of continuity of correspondance cannot be removed.[42]

In 1886, a question was raised by influential people residing in the Mofussil, who represented to the Dewan and the Civil Judge that great inconvenience was felt by litigants and witnesses owing to the Sub–divisional Courts having no power to entertain Rent and Small Cause Court suits of value higher than Rs. 500. The matter had also attracted the attention of the late Civil Judge, Rai Balaram Mallick Bahadur. The Civil Judge reported on this subject and moved the Council to extend the powers of sub – divisional Naib ahilkars. He was requested to prepare and submit a bill for the consideration of the Council.[43]

It was represented by an influential mohajan to the Dewan that the reduction of the period of limitation for rent suits and suits for recovery of debts from 12 to 3 years obliged land –lords and Mohajans to institute cases much more frequently than before, and that this proved injurious both to creditors and debtors. The subject was fully discussed in Council, and it was decided that no change should be made in the existing law of limitation.[44]

Kumar Gojendra Narayan, Assistant Civil Judge was authorized to sit both on the Executive and Judicial sides of the Council during Maharaja's absence. The number of sittings of the Council on the Judicial side under review was 19. There were 2 criminal appeals pending from the previous year and 5 were instituted during the year and also of these 2 only remained pending on the 31st March, 1888. Of 9 regular appeals for disposal, 4 remained pending at the close of the year and 3 miscellaneous cases remained undisposed of out of 10. Of 42 motions 25 remained pending.[45] The number of special appeals instituted during the year was 15 against 17 of the previous year. The total number for disposal was 34 of which 6 were decided. There was some interruption to the Council sittings during the year which partly accounts for the comparatively small number of cases disposed of. The Superintendent of the State went to Bombay to meet Maharaja on returning from England as also to Calcutta to meet the Maharaja's children. The Dewan was also absent on the same account and was besides on leave for two months. On the recommendation of the Civil judge the Council sanctioned for a further period of one year, the filling up by the legal petitioners &c., of the requisite particulars, names of parties and witnesses and the like in the forms of processes to be served on defendants and on witnesses.[46]

In 1888–89 The number of sittings of the Council on the Judicial side 25 during the year during report, against 19 of the previous year, at 2 of which Maharaja presided in person. Detailed statements containing particulars regarding disposal of cases were hereto appended. Two criminal appeals remained pending from the previous year and four were instituted during the year, of these two remained pending at the close of the year. Thirteen regular appeals remained pending on 31st March 1889, and eleven special appeals were disposed of during the year. Thirteen miscellaneous appeals and thirty–five motions remained pending at the close of the year. Most of the time of the Council, even on judicial days, was inevitably ocupied with discussions on the question of settlement and finance; hence fewer cases were disposed of than in normal times.[47] The Civil Judge recommended the insertion of a penal clause of the Patta Form prohibiting verbal settlement. The judge also suggested that the registation of Pattas, Kabulyats and deeds of relinquishment should be made compulsory, Section 17 of the Registration Act being amended to suit local requirements. The Dewan was requested to submit a report on the subject. The Vice –President in Council, with the previous sanction of Maharaja, ordered that the magisterial officers of the State should guide themselves by the provisions of Bengal Government Circular No. 35 J, dated 3rd August 1888, on the sibject of exemption of women from Medical examination without their consent. Regarding the practice of filling in by the legal practitioners &c. of the requisite particulars, names of parties, witnesses and the like in the forms of processes, having proved successful, the Vice–President in Council sanctioned the permanent adoption of the measure.[48]

During the year 1890, the Cooch Behar State Council

holds on the Legislative and Executive side 50 meetings of which 16 has been presided over by Maharaja. During that period the following themes were taken for grant :[49]

a) To constitute the infringement of private rights of fishery an offence, to render a trespass for the purposes of such infringement also an offence and to provide for punishment inrespect of the unlawful use of contrivances for the purpose of taking fish, the Dewan recommended the adoption by the State of the Private Fisheries Act, seeing that fishery in the State was not sufficiently or effectively protected under the existing law. The Bill was accordingly introduced.

b) To provide a law relating to fraudulent marks on merchandise in accordance (as far as local circumstances admit) with the law of British India, as enacted in the Merchandise Market Act of 1889, the Cooch Behar Merchandise Market Bill was introduced. This Bill adopted the provisions of the Merchandise Market Act with respect to false trade descriptions and recasted on the lines of that Act that part of the Indian Penal Code which relates to trade marks or property marks.

c) Some doubts were entertained as to the legality of the proceedings taken by the Settlement Officers under Act XX of 1848, which authorises officers exercising the powers of a Collecteor to impose fines. To remove misapprehension on the point, Maharaja in Council formally sanctioned the introduction of the Act and legalised all proceedings formerly taken in accordance with its spirit.

d) In several cases, the State Council experianced great inconvenience on account of the non–filing of attested copies of judgments in regular appeals. The Judicial Member therefore recommended the introduction in the State of Section 541 of Act XIV of 1882 (the new Civil Procedure Code), which makes the filing of attested copies of judgements obligatory (unless the Appellate Court dispenses therewith), as Act

VIII of 1859, which is in force in the State, appears to be silent on the point. The matter was represented to Maharaja and Maharaja accorded sanction to the adoption of the said section of the new Civil Procedure Code.

e) The laws of the State in regard to the registration, in India had reference only to power of attorney authorising agents to present documents for registration and admit execution thereof. For the convenience of the general public the provision of the law should have extended to all powers of attorney. Although the law of the State on the subject had a limited signification, the practice had always been to recognise all powers of attorney. Although the law of the State on the subject had a limited signification, the practice had always been to recognise all powers of attorney executed and registered in British India and subsequently registered here on payment of the usual stamp and registration fees. On the recommendation of the Council, Maharaja accorded sanction to the provisions of the law being extended to all powers of attorney with retrospective effect from the 29th June 1884.

f) On the recommendation of the Cooch Behar town Committee supported by the Council, Maharaja was pleased to accord sanction to Section 14 of the Cooch Behar Town Committee Act being so amended as to reduce the minimum number of meetings in a year to 8.

Regarding judicial matters the number of sittings of the State Council on the Judicial side was during the year as reported, 24 against 25 of the previous year. Detailed statements containing particulars regarding disposal of cases are hereto appended. Thirteen regular appeals remained pending from the previous year and five were instituted during the year; of these two were disposed of during the year.[50] All the Criminal appeals pending from the previous year and instituted during the year (7 in number) were disposed of during the year. There were 42 special appeals pending from the previous year and 20 were instituted during the year; of these 12 were disposed of during the year. Of the 56 motions for disposal, 14 were decided during the year. Nine out of 17 miscellaneous appeals remained pending at the close of the year.[51] In order to assist the Assitant Civil Judge who work had increased owing to the abolition of post of Sudder Naib Ahilkar, as also for the trial of rent suits, Maharaja in Council sanctioned the appointment of a Sub –Naib Ahilkar of the 2nd grade at the Sudder.

In 1898 – 99 records of the State shows that there were some legislative acts in the State, some of which were as follows :[52]

·Act V of 1898 —— The Bridge Tolls Act.

- Act IV of 1898 —— The Succession Certificate Act.
- Act of 1898 ——— An Act to amend the Cooch Behar Voluntary Under –tenures Act II of 1894.
- Act VII of 1898 —— An Act to amend the Cooch Behar Village Act III of 1893.
- Act III of 1898 ——— An Act to amend the Cooch Behar Revenue Act V of 1897.
- Act of 1899 —— An Act to provide punishment for cow-killing in the State.
- Act I of 1899 —— A Bill to Amend the Cooch Behar Limitation Act I of 1874.

In 1900 – 01 the following Act came into force :[53]

Act I of 1901 —— The Cooch Behar Telegraph Act.

Ther amendments of the Stamp Law, Rent Law, the Small Cause Court Act, Criminal Procedure Code and the Penal Code were still under consideration. The Law hitherto in force in the State has been governed by Bengal Regulation XIX of 1814, but as that was passed for separate estates and in some respects ill adapted to jotewari tenures, proposed to pass a short Act to meet the requirements of the State.[54]

There were 36 sittings on the judicial side of the Council

against 22 of the previous year. One regular appeal was pending from the previous year and two were instituted during the year; of which one was disposed of and two were pending at the close of the year.[55]

One criminal appeal was pending from the previous year and seven were instituted during the year under report; of which seven in all have been disposed of during the year under report. Seventeen special appeals were pending from the previous year and 14 were instituted during the year under report; 30 have been disposed of. Twenty–one motions were pending from the previous year and 43 were instituted during the year under report of which 59 were disposed of.[56] One miscellaneous appeal was instituted and disposed of during the year under report. Two miscellaneous cases were pending from the previous year and one was instituted during the year. All have been disposed of. One small cause Court reference was instituted and disposed during the year under record. The number of pending cases on the 31st March 1901 were 9 only against 42 of the same date in the previous year.[57]

The following table of 1901 – 02 shows the changes in the Subordinate Judicial posts:[58]

Act I of 1900 introducing with slight modifications the Civil Procedure Code (Act XIV of 1882) obtaining in British India came into force in the beginning of the year. The original suits instituted during the year four years are shown below :[59]

Sub Divisions	Names of officers	Terms of employment
Sudder	Gopal Chandra Chatterji, B.L.,Offg. Assistant Civil Judge	From the 1st April to the 26th of June 1901.
Sudder	Rajkrishna Das, L.C.E., Assistant Civil Judge	From the 27th of June 1901 to 31st March 1902
Sudder	Satis Chandra Mustafi , Sudder Rent Suit Officer	From the 1st April to the 31st of October 1901 and from the 17th December 1901 to the 31st of March 1902.
Toofangunj	Bama Charan Neogi, B.L., Offg. Naib Ahilkar	From the 1st April to 11th October 1901.
Toofangunj	Jagadballav Biswas,M.A.,B.L.,Offg. Naib Ahilkar	From 12th October to the 30th of November 1901.
Toofangunj	Padma Nath Das, Offg. Naib Ahilkar	From 1st of December to the 31st March 1902.
Dinhata	Ashutosh Ghosh, B.L., Naib Ahilkar	From the 1st April to the 18th November 1901 and from the 9th of February to the 31st march 1902.
Dinhata	Pramath Nath Chatterjee, M.A.,B.L.,offg. Naib Ahilkar	From the 19th November 1901 to the 8th February 1902.
Dinhata	Joy Gobinda Guha, B.L.,Offg. Sub Naib Ahilkar	From the 1st April to the 9th of August 1901.
Mathabhnaga	Hari Nath Basu, B.L., Naib Ahilkar	From the 10th August to the 30th of September 1901 and from the 14th of December 1901 to the 31st March of 1902.
Mathabhanga	Pramath Nath Chatterji, M.A.,B.L.,Offg. Naib Ahilkar	From the 1st April to the 1st of October 1901 and from the 6th December 1901 to the 31st of March 1902.
Mathabhanga	Narasimha Chandra Ghosh, M.A., B.L.,offg. Sub Naib Ahilkar	From the 2nd of October to the 14th of November 1901.
Mekhligunj	Padma Nath Das, B.L.,Naib Ahilkar	From the 1st April 1901 to the 31st of March 1902.
Mekhligunj	Bama Charan Neogi, B.L.,offg. Naib Ahilkar	From the 1st of April to the 16th of October 1901 From the 17th of October 1901 to the 31st of March 1902.

YEARS	*Civil suits and Rs. 50*	*Rent suits suits up to Rs. 20*	*Small cases Court*	*Total*
1898 – 99	3,081	5,794	1,455	10,330
1899 – 1900	2,254	5,351	1,744	9,349
1900 – 01	1,949	3,765	1,468	7,182

1901 – 02	1,501	3,882	1,494	6,577

It will be observed from the above that litigation has been steadily decreasing. This is due to the general well-being of the people and to the operation of the Kist and Sub in-feudation Acts.

The table given below shows the increase and decrease in the institutions in the several Civil and Rent Courts of the State :[60]

Courts	*CIVIL SUITS*		*RENT SUITS*	
	Increase	*Decrease*	*Increase*	*Decrease*
Civil Judge	——	8	——	1
Assistant Civil Judge	——	181	139	——
Naib Ahilkar, Toofangunj	——	78	61	——
Naib Ahilkar, Dinhata	——	154	——	116
Sub Naib Ahilkar, Dinhata	——	2	——	1
Naib Ahilkar, Mathabhanga	——	214	108	——
Sub Naib Ahilkar, Mathabhanga	——	10	6	——
Naib Ahilkar, Mekhligunj	——	75	——	79
Total	——	722	314	197

Civil suits decreased in the Courts of Civil and session Judge, the Assistant Civil Judge, the Naib Ahilkars of Toofangunj, Dinhata, Mathabhanga and Mekhligunj and the Sub – Naib Ahilkars of Dinhata and Mathabhanga by 8, 181, 78, 154, 214,75, 2 and 10 respectively.

Rent suits increased in the Courts of the Assistant Civil Judge, the Naib Ahilkars of Toofangunj and Mathabhanga the Sub Naib Ahilkars of Mathabhanga by 139, 61,108 and 6 respectively and decreased in the Courts of the Civil And Sessions Judge, the Naib Ahilkars of Dinhata and Mekhligunj and the sub–Naib Ahilkar of Dinhata nu 1, 116, 79 and 1 respectively. The increase was due to general causes.

The relation between landlords and tenants was not satisfactory. Instance of illegal exactions of Abwabs came to notice of the Revenue authorities and some of the jotedars were threatened with cancellation of their leases.

Statement No. 2 shows that out of a total of 6,577 institutions, 3,882 were rent suits, 2,394 suits on bond and other obligations 290 for land and other immoveable property and 11 relating to matrimonial rights.

The number of applications filed for execution of decrease during the last four years is shown in the table given below :[61]

YEARS	*Civil suits*	*Rent suits*	*Small cases Court suits up to Rs. 20 and Rs. 50*	*Total*
1898 – 99	2,396	2,108	763	5,267
1899 – 1900	2,388	2,055	772	5,215
1900 – 01	2,042	1,677	692	4,411
1901 – 02	1,656	1,554	623	3,833

The number of applications filed during the year was 3,833 against 4,411 tiled during the previous year, showing a decrease of 578 applications. The decrease was mainly due to the decrease in original suits.

The number of Miscellaneous cases of both Judicial and Non–Judicial nature instituted during the last two years is shown below :[62]

	Judicial	Non - Judicial
1900 – 01	571	16
1901 – 02	478	20

The number of applications for certificates of guardianship under Act VI of 1897 was 49 against 60 of the previous year, showing a decrease of 11 applications; and the number of applications for certificates under Act V of 1898 was 53 against 64 of the previous year, showing a decrease of 11 applications.

According to the number of original suits instituted, the several Subordinate Courts rank thus :[63]

- Assistant Civil Judge ———————— 1,823
- Naib, Ahilkar, Mathabhanga ———————— 1,705
- Ditto Dinhata ———————— 1,522

- Ditto Mekhligunj ———————— 838
- Ditto Toofangunj ———————— 634

The disposal of original suits during the last four years is shown in the statement given below :[64]

YEARS	*Civil suits*	*Rent suits*	*Small cases Court suits up to Rs. 20 and Rs. 50*	*Total*
1898 – 99	3,092	5,748	1,443	10,283
1899 – 1900	2,482	5,551	1,707	9,740
1900 – 1901	1,949	3,813	1,452	7,214
1901 – 1902	1,576	3,942	1,230	6,748

The total number of original suits disposed of was 6,748 against 7,214 of previous year, showing a decrease of 466 cases. The decrease was due to the decrease in the institutions.

According to disposals, the subordinate Courts rank thus :[65]

- Assistant Civil Judge ———————— 1,823
- Assistant Civil judge ———————— 1,047
- Sub Naib Ahilkar, Mathabhanga ———— 1,016
- Ditto Dinhata ———————— 953
- Naib Ahilkar, Mekhligunj ———————— 876
- Sudder Rent suit Officer ———————— 825
- Naib Ahilkar, Mathabhnaga ———————— 774
- Ditto Toofangunj ———————— 656
- Ditto Dinhata ———————— 584

The following table compares the number of regular contested suits for the last four years :[66]

YEARS	*No. of Civil suits*	*No. of Rent disposed of*	*Small cases Court suits disposed suits up to Rs. 20 of and Rs. 50*	*Total*
1898 – 99	591	839	198	1,236

1899 – 1900	525	859	228	1,607
1900 – 1901	470	604	240	1,314
1901 – 1902	442	574	207	1,223

The total number of contested cases decided was 1.223, being about 1/5 th of the entire number of disposals. With regard to the disposal of contested cases the Subordinate Courts rank thus :[67]

- Sub Naib Ahilkar ———————— 205
- Assistant Civil Judge ———————— 195
- Naib Ahilkar, Mathabhanga ———————— —168
- Naib Ahilkar, Dinhata ———————— 136
- Naib Ahilkar Toofangunj ———————— 133
- Sub Naib Ahilkar, Dinhata ———————— 131
- Naib Ahilkar, Mekhligunj ———————— 128
- Sudder Rent Suit Officer ———————— 115

The table given below shows the average duration of suits in each of the Subordinate Courts :[68]

Name of Courts	Civil Suits			Rent Suits			Small cases Court suits up to Rs. 20 and Rs. 50		
	Y	m	d	Y	m	d	Y	m	d
Assistant Civil Judge	0	6	14	0	2	23	0	2	0
Sudder Rent Suit Officer	------	------	------	0	3	23	------	------	------
Naib Ahilkar, Toofangunj	0	4	14	0	4	7	0	1	25
Naib Ahilkar, Dinhata	0	4	4	0	4	4	0	2	7
Naib Ahilkar, Mathabhanga	0	4	5	0	3	3	0	1	22
Naib Ahilkar Mekhligunj	0	3	6	0	3	17	0	1	12

Rs. 20 2,334 or a little more than 1/3 rd were for claims exceeding Rs. 20, but not exceeding Rs. 50; 1,342, or about 1/5 th were for claims exceeding Rs. 50, but not exceeding Rs. 100, but not exceeding Rs. 500; 32 cases were for claims exceeding Rs. 500 but not exceeding Rs. 1,000; 16 were for claims exceeding Rs. 1,000 but not exceeding Rs. 5000. One case was for claims exceeding Rs. 5000 but not exceeding Rs. 10,000.

The number of old cases pending at the end of the year wass 28 (4 pending over one year and 24 over six months0 against 26 of the previous year, showing an increase of 2 cases.

Babu Gopal Chandra Chatterji, B.L., Offg. Civil Judge and Babu Raj Krishna Das, I.C.E., Assistant Civil Judge and Babu Ashutosh Ghosh, B.L., and Hari Nath Basu,; Naib Ahilkar, tried small Cause Court suits up to Rs. 50 and all the other Naib Ahilkars up to Rs. 20 by summary procedure.

The statement given below shows the disposal of Execution cases during the last four years :[69]

YEARS	*Civil suits*	*Rent suits*	*Small cases Court suits up to Rs. 20 and Rs. 50*	*Total*
1898 – 99	2,401	2,052	767	5,220
1899 – 1900	2,408	2,153	788	5,349
1900 – 1901	2,199	1,797	699	5,695
1901 – 1902	1,663	1,488	645	3,796

The total number of Execution cases disposed of was 3,796 against 4,095 of the previous year, showing a decrease of 899 cases. There were 526 cases pending at the end of the year against 489 pending at the end of the year previous.

The table given below shows the disposal of Miscellaneous cases :[70]

	Judicial	*Non–Judicial*

Civil	321	19
Rent	112	—
Small cases Court suits up to Rs. 50 and Rs. 20	52	—
Total	485	19

The number of cases made over to the Civil Court Ameen for local inquiry by the different Civil Courts of the State was 103 against 81 cases of the previous year.This being added to 1 case pending at the close of the year previous, the total number for enquiry was 104. Of these, 96 cases were enquired into and 4 remained pending at the ned of the year. 4 cases were not enquired into for default of parties.

The Statement given below shows the work on the Civil original side of the Civil Judge's Court for last three years :[71]

Eleven original, 11 Execution and 17 Miscellaneous cases were pending at the close of the year.

The following table shows the total number of regular

Year	Original Suits				Execution				Miscellaneous			
	Pending from last year	Instituted or received by transfer	Disposed of	Pending	Pending from last year	Instituted or received by transfer	Disposed of	Pending	Pending from last year	Instituted or received by transfer	Disposed of	Pending
1899–1900	20	28	26	22	18	36	35	19	41	146	153	34
1900–1901	22	21	27	16	19	37	42	14	34	149	148	35
1901 - 1902	16	12	17	11	14	33	36	11	35	121	139	17

and miscellaneous appeals preferred to the Court during the last three years :[72]

1899 – 1900 ———————————— 191

1900 -1901 ———————————— 193

1901 – 1902 ———————————— 215

The number of appeals field during the year was 215 against 193 of the previous year, showing an increase of 22 appeals.

The result of appeals for the last three years is given in the table below :[73]

Year	No. of appeals for disposed	Confirmed	Reversed	Modified	Disposed of otherwise	Remarks
1899 – 1900	264	94	39	89	20	7
1900 – 1901	265	112	32	41	31	49
1901 – 1902	264	113	30	30	27	64

The following table shows the result of appeals against the decrease of each of the Subordinate Judicial Officers:[74]

The receipts of the Civil Department are shown below under several heads :

The following statement shows the stamp duty released

Name of Officers	Details of Disposals						Total disposed of	Remarks
	Confirmed	Reversed	Modified	Remanded	Disposed on default	Compromised		
Ashutosh Ghosh, B.L.	10	3	2	3	-----	-------	18	
Bama Charan Neogi, B.L.	9	3	5	1	2	------	20	
Gopal Chandra Chatterjee, B.L.	13	2	2	------	-----	4	21	
Hari Nath Basu, B.L.	22	3	7	1	2	------	35	
Joy Govinda Guha, B.L.	8	2	-----	1	-----	------	11	
Narasinha Ch. Ghosh, M.A., B.L.	24	8	6	3	2	------	43	
Padma Nath Das, B.L.	12	7	3	2	2	------	26	
Pramatha Nath Chatterjee, M.A.<B.L.	3	------	-----	-----	------	------	3	
Raj Krishna Das, L.C.E.	5	1	4	-----	------	------	10	
Rajanikanta Bhoumik, M.A., B.L.	3	------	------	-----	------	-------	3	
Satish Chandra Mustafi	4	1	1	-----	------	4	10	
Total	113	30	30	11	8	8	200	

during the year :[75]

1898 – 1899	Rs. 96,349
1899 – 1900	Rs. 84,780
1900 – 1901	Rs. 67,108
1901 – 1902	Rs. 62,164

The decrease of Rs. 4,914 was due to the decrease in the institution of suits.

The table given below shows the receipts of Ameen's fees under the head for the last four years :[76]

1898 – 1899	Rs. 759
1899 – 1900	Rs. 1,035
1900 – 1901	Rs. 567
1901 – 1902	Rs. 730

The amount of process fees &c. realized during the year was Rs. 16,409 against Rs. 18,260 of the previous year, showing a decrease of Rs. 1,851. The decrease was mainly due to the decrease in the institutions and in the realization of sale fees.

Fines and forfeitures : These amounted to Rs. 188 against Rs. 207 of the previous year, showing a decrease of Rs. 19.[77]

Other receipts including copying fees : These amounted to Rs. 3,840 against Rs. 3,495 of the previous year showing an increase of Rs. 345. This was mainly due to the increase in copying work.[78]

The total receipts under the above heads was Rs. 83,332 against Rs. 89,637 of the previous year, showing a decrease of Rs. 6,305.

Disbursement I — The salary of the judicial officers amounted to Rs. 17,298 against Rs. 17,036 of the previous year, showing an increase of Rs. 262. This was mainly due to the increase pay drawn throughout the year by the Civil and Session judge.[79]

II. Establishment charges : Amounted to Rs. 14, 757 against Rs. 14,361 of the previous year showing an increase of Rs. 396. This was chiefly due to the increment to the pay of Mohuris and others.[80]

III. Process Service —— The expenditure under this head was Rs. 7,985 against Rs. 7,849 of the previous year, showing an increase of Rs. 136. This was mainly due to the increment to the pay of the Nazir and the Naib Nazir.[81]

IV. Contingencies ———The amount expended under this head was Rs. 5,305 against Rs. 5,217 of the previous year, showing an increase of Rs. 88.[82]

V. Ameen's Salary ——— The cost of establishment of the Civil Court Ameen amounted to Rs. 873 against Rs. 837 of the previous year, showing an increase of Rs. 36.[83]

VI. Unforeseen ——— The amount expended under this head was Rs. 500 against Rs. 9 of the previous year, showing an increase of Rs. 491. Rs. 500 was met from this head towards part payment of the price of a pair of horses for the Civil and Session Judge.[84]

Total amount of expenditure amounted to Rs. 46,719 against Rs.45,308 of the previous year, showing an increase of Rs.1,411.

The net receipts of the Civil Department amounted to Rs. 36,613 against Rs. 44,329 of the previous year, showing a decrease of Rs. 7,716.

Total amount of fees realized during the year was Rs. 3,437 – 11 against Rs. 3,196 of the previous, showing an increase of Rs. 241 – 11. Out of the total receipts Rs. 1,562 – 9 were credited to the State and the balance, Rs. 1,875 – 2 distributed among the copyists.[85]

The following statement shows the number of copyists employed in each Court with their average monthly income:[86]

Name of Courts	No. of copyrights	No. of comparing clerks	Average monthly income of each copyright	Remarks
	(a)		Rs. A. P.	
Sudder ----------	4	1 (b)	19 9 2	(a)There was formally a copyist one more was appointed from December 1901 (b) The work was carried on by the regular staff without any remuneration
Toofangunj ------	1	-------	6 5 10	
Dinhata -----------	2	1	15 15 9	
Mathabhanga ----	8	1 (b)	12 2 4	
Mekhligunj -------	2	-------	• 9 4	Ditto

Courts	*Civil*	*Rent*	*Total*
Civil Judge Court	191	62	253
Assistant Civil Judge's Court	1,094	542	1,636
Sudder Rent Suit Court	———	1,554	1,554
Mathabhanga	806	1,341	2,147
Total	2,091	3,499	5,590

The table given below shows the records of cases destroyed during the year :[88]

Courts. Description of records destroyed.

Dinhata ———————— B File of Rent original suits from February to September 1891.

(Naib Ahilkar's Court)

Mathabhanga ———————— B File of Civil original suits from April 1890 to December 1897.

(Naib Ahilkar's Court)

———————— B File of Civil original suits from May 1890 to December 1891.

(Sub-Naib Ahilkar's Court)

———————— B File of Rent original suits from April 1890 to December 1897.

———————— B File of Rent Execution cases from April 1890 to March 1897.

Mekhligunj ——————— B File of Civil Original suits from April 1893 to December, 1896.

Similarly the Annual Statement of 1902–03 shows a graphic picture on the administration of Civil Justice. According to the Superintendant of the State there were a number of statements has been included on the year which were as follows :

The following table shows the changes in the subordinate Judicial posts :[89]

The original suits instituted during the last four years

Sub Divisions	Names of officers	Terms of employment
Sudder ———————	Rajkrishna Das, L.C.E., Assistant Civil Judge	From the 1st April 1902 to the 31st of March 1903.
Sudder ———————	Satis Chandra Mustafi , Sudder Rent Suit Officer	Ditto Ditto
Toofangunj ———————	Padma Nath Das, Offg. Naib Ahilkar	Ditto Ditto
Dinhata ———————	Ashutosh Ghosh, B.L., Naib Ahilkar	Ditto Ditto
Dinhata ———————	Rajani kanta Bowmick, M.A., B.L., Sub Naib Ahilkar	Ditto Ditto
Mathabhnaga ———————	Hari Nath Basu, B.L.,Naib Ahilkar	Ditto Ditto
Mathabhanga ———————	Narasinha Chandra Ghosh, M.A., B.L., Sub Naib Ahilkar	From the 1st April to the 10th November 1902 and from the 11th of December to the 31st march 1903.
Mekhligunj ———————	Bama Charan Neogi, B.L.,offg. Naib Ahilkar	From the 1st April to the 3rd of July 1902 and from the 15th December 1902 to 31st March 1903.
Mekhligunj ———————	Gopal Chandra Chatterjee, B.L., Naib Ahilkar	From the 4th July to the 14th of December1902.

YEARS	*Civil suits*	*Rent suits*	*Small cases Court suits up to Rs. 20 and Rs. 50*	*Total*
1899 – 1900	2,254	5,351	1,744	9,349
1900 – 01	1,949	3,765	1,468	7,182
1901 – 02	1,501	3,882	1,194	6,577
1902 – 03	1,680	4,767	1,331	7,778

It will be observed from the above that the number of institutions during the year under report was 7,778 against 6,577 of the previous year. The increase is mainly due to the introduction from the 1st of April 1903 of the new Stamp act (I of 1903) prescribing increased duties for plaints.

The table given below shows the increase and decrease in the institutions in the several Civil and Rent Courts of the State :[91]

Courts	*CIVIL SUITS*		*RENT SUITS*	
	Increase	*Decrease*	*Increase*	*Decrease*
Civil Judge	4	——	——	——
Assistant Civil Judge	57	——	199	——
Sudder Rent Suit Officer	——	——	——	3
Naib Ahilkar, Toofangunj	15	——	——	10
Naib Ahilkar, Dinhata	69	——	195	——
Sub Naib Ahilkar, Dinhata	7	——	——	7
Naib Ahilkar, Mathabhanga	67	——	295	——
Sub Naib Ahilkar, Mathabhanga	2		——	9
Naib Ahilkar, Mekhligunj	95	——	225	——
Total	316	——	914	29

Civil Suits increased in the Courts of the Civil and Session Judge, the Assistant Civil Judge, the Naib Ahilkars of Toofangunj, Dinhata, Mathabhanga and Mekhligunj and the Sub Naib Ahilkars of Dinhata and Mathabhanga by 4,57,15,69,67,95,7 and 2 respectively.

Rent suit increased in the courts of the Assistant Civil Judge and the Naib Ahilkars of Dinhata, Mathabhanga and Mekhligunj by 199, 195, 295 and 225 respectively and decreased in the Courts of the Naib Ahilkar of Toofangunj, the Sudder Rent Suit Officer and the Sub–Naib Ahilkars of Dinhata and Mathabhanga by 10, 3,7 and 9 respectively.[92]

Statement No. 2 shows that out of a total of 7,778 institutions, 4,767 were rent suits, 2,657 were suits on bond and other obligations, 336 for land and other immoveable property and 18 relating to matrimonial rights.

The number of applications filed for execution of decrees during the last four years is shown in the table given below :[93]

YEAR	*Civil*	*Rent*	*Small Cause Court*	*Total*
1899 – 1900	2,388	2,055	772	5,215
1900 – 1901	2,042	1,677	692	4,411
1901 – 1902	1,656	1,554	623	3,833
1902 – 1903	1,539	1,540	650	3,729

The number of applications filed during the year was 3,729 against 3,833 filed during the previous year, showing a decrease of 104 applications.

The number of Miscellaneous cases instituted during the last two years is shown below :[94]

Years	*Judicial*	*Non–Judicial*
1901 – 1902	478	20
1902–03	463	16

The number of applications for certificates of guardianship under Act VI of 1897 was 48 against 49 of the previous year, showing a decrease of one case and the number of applications for certificates under Act V of 1898 was 40 against 53 of the previous year, showing a decrease of 13 applications.

According to the number of original suits instituted the subordinate courts rank thus :[95]

- Assistant Civil Judge ———————— 2,079

- Naib Ahilkar, Mathabhanga —————— 2,067
- Ditto. Dinhata —————— 1,768
- Ditto Mekhligunj —————— 1,158
- Ditto Toofangunj —————— 639

The disposal of original suits during the last four years shown in the statement given below :[96]

YEAR	*Civil*	*Rent*	*Small Cause Court*	*Total*
1899 – 1900	2,482	5,551	1,707	9,740
1900 – 1901	1,949	3,813	1,452	7,214
1901 – 1902	1,576	3,942	1,230	6,748
1902 – 1903	1,540	4,413	1,279	7,232

The total number of original suits disposed of was 7,232 against 6,748 of the previous year, showing an increase of 484 cases. To evade the provisions of the New Stamp Act, a large number of suits were instituted towards the close of the year and these could not be disposed of during the period.

According to disposals, the subordinate courts rank thus :[97]

- Sub Naib Ahilkar, Mathabhanga —————— 1,084
- Sudder Rent Suit Officer —————— 1,079
- Sub – Naib Ahilkar, Dinhata —————— 1,005
- Assistant Civil Judge —————— 916
- Naib Ahilkar, Mekhligunj —————— 914
- Ditto. Mathabhanga —————— 896
- Ditto. Dinhata —————— 721
- Ditto. Toofangunj —————— 606

The following table compares the number of regular contested suits for the last four years :[98]

Year dsposed of	*No. of Civil suits disposed of and Rs. 50*	*No. of Rent suits suits up to Rs. 20*	*Small cases Court*	*Total*

1899 – 1900	525	859	223	1,607
1900 – 1901	470	604	240	1,314
1901 – 1902	442	574	207	1,223
1902 – 1903	446	568	199	1,213

The total number of contested cases decided was 1,213 being about 1/6 th of the entire number of disposals.

With regard to the disposal of contested cases, the subordinate courts rank thus :[99]

- Assistant Civil Judge ———— 198
- Naib Ahilkar, Mathabhanga ———— 171
- Sub Naib Ahilkar, Dinhata ———— 159
- Naib Ahilkar, Dinhata ———— 147
- Sub Naib Ahilkar, Mathabhanga ———— 142
- Sudder Rent Suit Officer ———— 138
- Naib Ahilkar, Mekhligunj ———— 137
- Naib Ahilkar, Toofangunj ———— 114

The table given below shows the average duration of suits in each of the subordinate courts :[100]

Name of Courts	Civil Suits			Rent Suits			Small cases Court suits up to Rs. 20 and Rs. 50		
	Y	m	d	Y	m	d	Y	m	d
Assistant Civil Judge	0	7	4	0	5	16	0	2	5
Sudder Rent Suit Officer	----	----	----	0	3	28	----	----	----
Toofangunj	0	4	12	0	4	3	0	1	27
Dinhata	0	6	0	0	3	29	0	1	25
Mathabhanga	0	3	15	0	2	8	0	1	10
Mekhligunj	0	3	15	0	3	17	0	1	12

2,347 or a little less than one –third were for claims not exceeding Rs. 20; 2,495 or a little more than one –third were for claims exceeding Rs. 20 but not exceeding Rs. 50;

1,522 or a little more than one–fifth were for claims exceeding Rs. 50 but not exceeding Rs. 100; 825 or a little more than one–eighth were for claims exceeding Rs. 100 but not exceeding Rs. 500; 32 cases were for claims exceeding Rs. 500 but not exceeding Rs. 1000; 11 were for claims exceeding Rs. 1,000 but not exceeding Rs. 5,000. There was no case for claims exceeding Rs. 10,000.[101]

The number of old cases pending at the end of the year was 36 (6 pending over one year and 30 over six months) against 28 of the previous year, showing an increase of 8 cases.

The statement given below shows that the disposal of Execution cases during the last four years :[102]

YEARS	*Civil suits*	*Rent suits*	*Small Causes Court*	*Total*
1899 – 1900	2,408	2,453	788	5,349
1900 – 1901	2,199	1,797	699	4,695
1901 – 1902	1,663	1,488	646	3,796
1902 – 1903	1,531	1,596	621	3,748

The total number of Execution cases disposed of was 3,748 against 3,796 of the previous year, showing a decrease of 48 cases only. There were 507 cases pending at the end of the year against 526 pending at the end of the year previous.

The table given below shows the disposal of Miscellaneous cases :[103]

	Judicial	*Non-Judicial*
Civil—	289	15
Rent—	123	——
Small Cases Court suits upto Rs. 50 and Rs. 20	45	——
Total	457	15

The number of cases made over to the Civil Court Ameen for local enquiry by the different Civil Courts of the state was 116 against 103 cases of the previous year. This being added to 4 cases pending at the close of the year previous, the total number for enquiry was 120. Of these 115 were enquired into and 5 remained pending at the end of the year.

The statement given below shows the work on the Civil original side of the Civil judge's Court for the last three years :[104]

Year	Original Suits				Execution				Miscellaneous			
	Pending from last year	Instituted or received by transfer	Disposed of	Pending	Pending from last year	Instituted or received by transfer	Disposed of	Pending	Pending from last year	Instituted or received by transfer	Disposed of	Pending
1900 – 1901	22	21	27	16	19	37	42	14	34	149	148	35
1901 – 1902	16	12	17	11	14	33	36	11	35	121	139	17
1902 – 1903	11	16	11	16	11	23	29	05	17	107	97	27

Sixteen original, 5 execution and 27 Miscellaneous cases were pending at the close of the year.

the last three years :[105]

1900 – 1901 ———————————— 193

1901 – 1902 ———————————— 215

1902 – 1903 ———————————— 193

The number of appeals filed during the year was 193 against 215 of the previous year, showing a decrease of 22 appeals.

The result of the appeals for the last three years is given in the table below :[106]

Year	*No. of*	*Confirmed*	*Reversed*	*Modified*	*Disposed of*	*Pending*

	appeals for disposed				otherwise	
1900 – 1901	265	112	32	41	31	49
1901 – 1902	264	113	30	30	27	64
1902 – 1903	257	126	34	20	22	55

There were 257 appeals for disposal including those remained pending at the close of the year previous. Of these 202 were disposed of and 55 remained pending.

The following table shows the result of appeals against the decrees of each of the Subordinate Judicial Officers:[107]

Name of Officers	Details of Disposals						Total disposed of	Remarks
	Confirmed	Reversed	Modified	Remanded	Disposed on default	Compromised		
Ashutosh Ghosh, B.L.	12	1	2	1	----	-----	16	
Bama Charan Neogi, B.L.	6	1	----	----	----	-----	7	
Gopal Chandra Chatterjee, B.L.	6	----	1	-----	----	----	7	
Hari Nath Basu, B.L.	25	8	2	4	----	-----	39	
Narasinha Ch. Ghosh, M.A., B.L.	18	5	3	1	1	1	29	
Padma Nath Das, B.L.	12	7	2	1	1	1	24	
Pramatha Nath Chatterjee, M.A.B.L.	3	-----	1	-----	----	-----	4	
Raj Krishna Das, L.C.E.	28	7	4	5	1	2	47	
Rajani kanta Bhoumik, M.A., B.L.	10	4	1	2	1	-----	18	
Satish Chandra Mustafi	6	1	4	----	-----	-----	11	
Total	126	34	20	14	4	4	202	

Stamp Duty ——— The following statement shows the stamp duty realized during the last four years :[109]

1899 -1900 ——— 84,780

1900 -1901 ——— 67,108

1901 -1902 ——— 62,164

1902 – 1903 ——————————————— 67,786

The increase of Rs. 5,622 was due to the increase in the number of institutions.

Ameen's fees ——————— The table given below shows the receipts under this head for the last four years :[110]

1899 -1900 ——————————————— Rs. 1,035

1900 -1901 ——————————————— Rs. 567

1901 -1902 ——————————————— Rs. 730

1902 -1903 ——————————————— Rs. 783

Process fees ——— The amount of process fees realized during the year was Rs. 16,679 against Rs. 16,409 of the previous year, showing an increase of Rs 270 only.

Fines and forfeitures ——— These amounted to Rs. 277 against Rs. 188 of the previous year, showing an increase of Rs. 88 only.

Other receipts including copying fees ——— These amounted to Rs. 3,871 against Rs. 3,840 of the previous year, showing an increase of Rs. 31 only.

The total receipts under the above heads were Rs. 89,396 against Rs. 83,332 of the previous year, showing an increase of Rs. 6,064.

Disbursement I — The salary of the judicial officers amounted to Rs. 17,754 against Rs. 17,208 of the previous year, showing an increase of Rs. 262. This was mainly due to the increase pay drawn throughout the year by the Civil and Session judge.[111]

II. Establishment charges : Amounted to Rs. 14, 858 against Rs. 14,757 of the previous year showing an increase of Rs. 101. This was chiefly due to the increment to the pay of Mohuris.[112]

III. Process Service —— The expenditure under this head was Rs. 8,074 against Rs. 7,985 of the previous year, showing an increase of Rs. 89.[113]

IV. Contingencies ———The amount expended under this head was Rs. 5,299 against Rs. 5,305 of the previous year, showing an increase of Rs. 88.[114]

V. Ameen's Salary ——— The cost of establishment of the Civil Court Ameen amounted to Rs. 870 against Rs. 873 of the previous year, showing a decrease of Rs. 3.[115]

VI. Unforeseen ——— The amount expended under this head was Rs. 499 – 3 against Rs. 500 of the previous year. Of this Rs. 137 – 3 was expended on the purchase of uniforms of 2 Chopdars who accompanied the Civil Judge to the Delhi Durbar and Rs. 362 was met towards the part payment of the price of horses for the Judge.[116]

Total amount of expenditure amounted to Rs. 47,353 against Rs.46,719 of the previous year, showing an increase of Rs.634.

The net receipts of the Civil Department amounted to Rs. 42,043 against Rs. 36,613 of the previous year, showing an increase of Rs. 5,430.

Total amount of fees realized during the year was Rs. 3,517 against Rs. 3,437 – 11 of the previous, showing an increase of Rs. 79 – 5. Out of the total receipts Rs. 1,613 – 4 was credited to the State and the balance, Rs. 1,903 – 12 distributed among the copyists.[117]

The following statement shows the number of copyists employed in each court with their average monthly income:[118]

Name of Courts	No. of copyrights	No. of comparing clerks	Average monthly income of each copyright	Remarks
			Rs. A. P.	
Sudder ----------	4	1	17 2 0	
Toofangunj -------	1	(a) --------	6 11 0	(a) The work was carried on by the regular staff without any remuneration
Dinhata -----------	2	1	15 9 1	
Mathabhanga ----	3	1 (a)	----------------	
Mekhligunj -------	2	--------	• 4 11	

Courts	*Civil*	*Rent*	*Total*
Civil Judge Court	347	66	413
Assistant Civil Judge's Court	970	172	1,142
Sudder Rent Suit Court	———	1,435	1,435
Toofangunj	1,298	770	2,068
Dinhata	1,154	2,001	3,155
Mathabhanga	721	837	1,558
Mekhligunj	1,355	2,038	3,393
Total	5,845	7,319	13,164

List of Judicial and revenue divisions of Cooch Behar State in 1902 – 03 :[120]

(A.)

Name of Divisions	*Name of Police Station each*	*Area in square miles*	*Population*
Sudder Sub Division	Kotwali Station	284	1,21,609
Toofangunj	Fulbari Station	223	73,438
Dinhata	Dinhata Station	269	1,43,900
Mathabhanga	Mathabhanga Station	334	1,40,183
	Sitalkuchi Station		
Mekhligunj	Mekhligunj Station	197	87,843

(B.)

Return showing the number of Civil and Rent Courts of the Cooch Behar State for the year 1902 -1903 :[121]

CIVIL		*RENT*		*TOTAL*
Appellate	*Original*	*Appellate*	*Original*	
1	13	1	9	24

In 1905 the Council held 48 sittings against 21 of the previous year. The following table shows the work done by the State Council on its judicial side :[122]

During the year under report Act II of 1904 (The Cooch Behar Village Chaukidari Amendment Act) was passed

Natures of cases	Pending at the beginning of the year	Installed during the year	Total	DISPOSED OF									Pending at the close of the year
				Received	Modified	Confirmed	Struck off	Remanded	Compromised	Rejected	Granted	Total	
CIVIL													
Regular appeals	8	2	5	-----	---	4	-----	-----	-----	-----	---	4	1
Special appeals	17	12	29	4	---	24	-----	----	-----	-----	-----	28	1
Miscellaneous appeals	4	3	7	4	----	3	-----	-----	-----	-----	---	7	-----
Motions, etc.	15	8	23	-----	-----	-----	---	-----	---	21	2	23	-----
Miscellaneous	-----	1	1	-----	---	-----	---	---	-----	-----	1	1	-----
cases	6	3	9	1	---	8	----	----	-----	---	---	9	-----
Small Cause Court Reference	2	-----	2	----	----	-----	-----	-----	-----	1	1	2	----
RENT													
Special appeals	------	2	2	----	----	2	-----	-----	---	-----	----	2	-----
REVENUE			3	----	----	3	-----	---	-----	-----	-----	3	-----
Motions, etc.	2	1	8	3									
CRIMINAL		6										8	-----
Appeals	1	9	10	---	----	7	-----	-----	-----	6	2	10	-----
Motions	8	9	17	----	----	-----	- -----	-----	---	13	3	16	1
TOTAL	60	56	116	12	---	51	----	----	----	41	9	113	3

and a Bill (No. III of 1904) to Amend the Cooch Behar Stamp Act I of 1903, was introduced. In exercise of the powers conferred by sections 5 (b), 59,61, 62, 66 and 76 of the Cooch Behar Stamp Act I of 1903, the State Council promulgated certain rules under the Act.[123]

The office of the Civil and Session Judge throughout the year 1906 -07 shows the following the statement of their terms of employment :[124]

Sub Divisions	*Names of officers*	*Terms of employment*
Sudder	Rajkrishna Das, L.C.E., Assistant Civil Judge	From the 1st April 1902 to the14th of September 1906 from the 27th of October 1906 to the 31st of March 1907.
Sudder	Rai Choudhuri Satish Chandra Mustafi, Rent Suit Officer	From the 1st April to 6th of April 1906.
Sudder	Pramatha Nath Chatterjee, M.A.,B.L.,Rent Suit Officer	From the 7th of April 1906 to the 31st of March 1907.
Sudder	Narasinha Chandra Ghosh, M.A.,B.L., Rent suit Naib Ahilkar	From the 1st to the 6th of April 1906`
Sudder	Rajani Kanta Bhowmik, M.A., B.L.,Additional Sudder Rent Suit Sub Naib Ahilkar	From the 10th April to the 20th of September 1906.
Sudder	Jotindra Mohan Sen Gupta, B.L., Additional Sudder Rent Suit Naib Ahilkar	From the 1st of April to the 11th of June 1906.
Toofangunj	Narasinha Chandra Ghosh, M.A.,B.L., Offg. Naib Ahilkar	From the 12th of June 1906 to the 31st of March 1907.
Toofangunj	Rai Chowdhuri Satish Chandra Mustafi, Naib Ahilkar	From the 1st to 9th April 1906 and from the 21st of September 1906 to the 31st of March 1907.
Dinhata	Gopal Chandra Chatterjee, B.L., Naib Ahilkar	From the 10th of April to the 20th September 1906.
Dinhata	Jotindra Mohan Sen Gupta, B.L.,Sub Naib Ahilkar	From the 1st of April to the 23rd of June 1906 and from the 4th of July 1906 to the 31st of March 1907.

Dinhata Uma Nath Dutta, B.L., Offg. From the 5th of May to the 2nd
Sub Naib Ahilkar June 1906.

Mathabhanga Ashutosh Ghosh, B.L., Naib From the 23rd of June to the 5th
Ahilkar of July 1906 and from
the 23rd of August
1906 to the 31st of
March 1907.

Mathabhanga Jatindra Mohan Sen Gupta, From the 1st of April 1906 to
the
B.L., Sub Naib Ahilkar
31st of March 1907.

Mathabhanga Uma Nath Dutta, B.L., Offg. From the 1st of April to the 4th
Naib Ahilkar of May 1906.

Mathabhanga Bama Charan Neogi, B.L., From the 9th of July to the 20th
Sub Naib Ahilkar of August 1906.

Mekhligunj Hari Nath Basu, B.L, Naib From the 21st of August 1906
to
Ahilkar the 31st of March
1907From the
1st of April 1906 to
the 31st of
March
1907.

The original suits instituted during the four years are shown below :[125]

Years	*Civil suits*	*Rent suits*	*Small causes Court suits up to Rs. 20 and Rs. 50*	*Total*
1903 – 04	1,406	3,574	1,251	6,231
1904 – 05	1,476	4,244	1,296	7,016
1905 – 06	1,534	3,881	1,628	7,043
1906 – 07	1,689	3,269	1,617	6,575

It will be observed from the above that the number of institutions during the year under record was 6,575 against 7,043 of the previous year, showing a decrease of 468 suits. Civil suits increased by 144 and rent suits decreased by 612. The net decrease was due to high prices, specially of jute.

The table given below shows the increase and decrease in the institutions in the several Civil and Rent Courts of the State :[126]

Courts	*Civil Suits*	*Rent Suits*

	Increase	Decrease	Increase	Decrease
Civil Judge	7	—	—	1
Assistant Civil Judge	106	—	—	162
Sudder Rent Suit Officer	—	—	1	—
Naib Ahilkar, Toofangunj	2	—	—	71
Naib Ahilkar, Dinhata	—	18	—	159
Sub Naib Ahilkar, Dinhata	4	—	5	—
Naib Ahilkar, Mathabhanga	70	—	—	158
Sub Naib Ahilkar Mathabhanga	—	—	—	2
Naib Ahilkar ,Mekhligunj	—	27	—	65
Total	189	45	6	618

Civil suits increased in the courts of the Civil judge, the Assistant Civil Judge, the Naib Ahilkars of Toofangunj and Mathabhanga and the Sub Naib Ahilkar of Dinhata by 7, 106, 2,70 and 4 respectively and decreased in the courts of the Naib Ahilkars of Dinhata and Mekhligunj by 18 and 27 respectively.

Rent suit increased in the Courts of the Sudder Rent Suit Officers and the Sub Naib Ahilkar of Dinhata by 1 and 5 respectively and decreased in the Courts of the Civil Judge and Assistant Civil Judge and Assistant Civil Judge, the Naib Ahilkars of Toofangunj, Dinhata, Mathabhanga and Mekhligunj and the Sub Naib Ahilkar of Mathabhanga by 1, 162, 71, 159, 158, 65 and 2 respectively.

Statement No.2 shows that out of a total of 6,575 institutions, 3,267 were rent suits, 2934 were suits on bonds and other obligations, 364 for land and other immoveable properties and 10 relating to matrimonial rights.

The number of applications for execution of decrees during the last four years is shown in the table given below :[127]

YEAR	Civil	Rent	Small Cause Court	Total
1903 – 1904	1,490	1,413	607	3,510
1904 – 1905	1,427	1,444	592	3,463

1905 – 1906	1,416	1,678	716	3,810
1906 – 1907	1,333	1,436	635	3,404

The number of applications filed during the year was 3,404 against 3,810 of the previous year, showing a decrease of 406 applications.

The number of miscellaneous cases instituted during the last two years is shown below :[128]

Years	*Judicial*	*Non–Judicial*
1905–1906	469	27
1906–1907	464	23

The number of applications for certificates of guardianship under Act VI of 1897 was 50 against 47 of the previous year showing an increase of 3 applications and the number of applications for certificates under Act V of 1898 was 60 against 55 of the previous year, showing an increase of 5 applications.

According to the number of original suits instituted, the Subordinate Courts rank thus :[129]

- Assistant Civil Judge — 1,867
- Naib Ahilkar, Mathabhanga — 1,755
- Ditto Dinhata — 1,454
- Ditto Mekhligunj — 878
- Ditto Toofangunj — 567

The disposal of original suits during the last four years is shown in the statement given below :[130]

YEAR	*Civil*	*Rent*	*Small Cause Court*	*Total*
1903 – 1904	1,546	3,907	1,287	6,740
1904 – 1905	1,466	4,261	1,246	6,991
1905 – 1906	1,533	3,845	1,624	7,002
1906 – 1907	1,598	3,287	1,610	6,495

The total number of original suits disposed of was 6,495 against 7,002 of the previous year, showing a decrease of 507 suits. The decrease was due to decrease of institutions.

According to disposals, the Subordinate Courts rank thus :[131]

- Assistant Civil Judge ———————— 968
- Naib Ahilkar, Mathabhanga ———————— 900
- Naib Ahilkar, Mekhligunj ———————— 880
- Sudder Rent Suit Officer ———————— 855
- Sub Naib Ahilkar, Dinhata ———————— 798
- Sub Naib Ahilkar, Mathabhnaga ———————— 779
- Naib Ahilkar, Dinhata ———————— 732
- Naib Ahilkar, Mathabhanga ———————— 563

The following table compares the number of contested original suits for the last four year :[132]

YEAR	*Civil*	*Rent*	*Small Cause Court*	*Total*
1903 – 1904	392	491	196	1,079
1904 – 1905	356	407	192	1,015
1905 – 1906	379	454	280	1,113
1906 – 1907	451	399	254	1,104

The total number of contested suits decided was 1,104, being more than one-sixth of the entire number of disposal.

With regard to the disposal of contested suits, the subordinate Courts rank thus :[133]

- Assistant Civil Judge ———————— 226
- Naib Ahilkar, Mathabhanga ———————— 183
- Naib Ahilkar, Mekhligunj ———————— 142
- Naib Ahilkar, Dinhata ———————— 133
- Sub Naib Ahilkar, Mathabhanga ———————— 116

Name of Courts	Civil Suits		Rent Suits		Small cases Court suits	
	Contested	Uncontested	Contested	Uncontested	Contested	Uncontested
	m. d.	m. d.	m. d.	m. d.	m. d.	m. d.
Assistant Civil Judge	5 8	1 11	———	1 19	1 2	0 10
Sudder Rent Suit Courts	———	———	• 12	2 4	———	———
Toofangunj Court	3 8	1 9	3 6	1 4	1 2	1 2
Dinhata Court	4 0	0	3 6	1 2	1	0 25
Mathabhanga Court	4 27	27	2 2	1 0	6	0 25
Mekhligunj Court	2 19	0	1 22	0	1	0 18
		21		27	2	
		0			0	
		29			24	

The duration was longest in the Court of the Assistant Civil Judge and shortest in that of Mekhligunj.

Out of the total number of original suits disposed of 1,747 or less than one –third were for claims not exceeding Rs. 20; 2,247 or more than one –third were for claims exceeding Rs. 20 but not exceeding Rs. 50; 1,374 or less than one –forth were for claims exceeding Rs. 100 but not exceeding Rs. 500; 37 were for claims exceeding Rs. 500 but not exceeding Rs. 1000; 19 were for claims exceeding Rs. 1000 but not exceeding Rs. 5,000. There was only one suit exceeding Rs. 10,000.

The number of old suits pending at the end of the year was 27 (19 pending over 6 months and 8 pending over one year) against 22 of the previous year.

Raj Krishna Das, I.C.E., Assistant Civil judge and Gopal Chandra Chatterjee, B.L., Ashutosh Ghosh, B.L., and Hari nath Basu, B.L., Naib Ahilkar, tried small Court Suits up to Rs. 50 and all other Naib Ahilkars up to Rs. 20 by summary procedure.

The statement given below shows the disposal of Execution cases during the last four year :[135]

YEAR	*Civil*	*Rent*	*Small Cause Court*	*Total*
1903 – 1904	1,500	1,429	629	3,558
1904 – 1905	1,441	1,413	596	3,450
1905 – 1906	1,415	1,671	690	3,776
1906 – 1907	1,371	1,460	651	3,482

The total number of execution cases disposed of was 3,482 against 3,776 of the previous year, showing a decrease of 294 cases. There were 428 cases pending at the close of the year against 506 pending at the end of the previous year.

The table given below shows the disposal of miscellaneous cases :[136]

	Judicial	*Non-Judicial*
Civil————	283	23
Rent————	122	——
Small cause cases suits up to Rs. 20 and Rs. 50	47	——
Total————	452	23

The number of cases made over to the Civil Court Ameen for local enquiry by the different Civil Courts of the State was 114 against 118 made over during the previous

Years	Original Suits				Execution				Miscellaneous			
	Pending from last year	Instituted or received by transfer	Disposed of	Pending	Pending from last year	Instituted or received by transfer	Disposed of	Pending	Pending from last year	Instituted or received transfer	Disposed of	Pending
1904–05	11	22	17	16	12	30	34	8	34	102	121	15
1905–06	16	18	19	15	8	18	17	9	15	112	104	23
1906-07	15	24	20	19	9	22	24	8	23	122	122	23

year. Only one of these cases remained pending inquiry at the close of the year.

The statement given below shows the work on the Original Civil side of the Civil Judge's Court for the last three years :[137]

Nineteen Original, 8 Execution and 23 Miscellaneous cases were pending at the close of the year.

The following table shows the total number of regular and miscellaneous appeals preferred to the Court during the last three year :[138]

1904 – 1905 ———— 154

1905 – 1906 ———— 150

1906 – 1907 ———— 157

(a) The number of appeals filed during the year was 157 against 150 of the previous year, showing an increase of 7 appeals:[139]

Year	*No. of appeals for disposed*	*Confirmed*	*Reversed*	*Modified*	*Disposed of otherwise*	*Pending*
1904 – 1905	206	101	28	16	21	40
1905 – 1906	190	89	32	13	15	41

Name of Officers	Details of Disposals						Total disposed of	Remarks
	Confirmed	Reversed	Modified	Remanded	Disposed on default	Compromised		
	23	5	1	----	----	1	30	
Raj Krishna Das, L.C.E.	13	2	3	----	1	----	19	
Gopal Chandra Chatterjee, B.L.	11	4	----	1	----	----	16	
Ashutosh Ghosh, B.L.	22	7	2	----	2	----	33	
Hari Nath Basu, B.L.	3	2	2	----	----	----	7	
Rai Choudhuri Satish Chandra Mustafi	1	1	----	1	----	----	3	
Bama Charan Neogi, B.L.	1	1	----	----	----	----	2	
Pramatha Nath Chatterjee, M.A.,B.L.	6	2	----	1	----	----	9	
Narasinha Chandra Ghosh, M.A., B.L	8	2	1	----	1	----	12	
Uma Nath Dutt, B.L.	4	4	----	----	----	----	8	
Total	92	30	9	3	4	1	139	

1906 – 1907	198	92	30	9	8	59

There were 198 appeals for disposal including those which remained pending at the end of the year previous. Of these, 139 were disposed of and 59 remained pending.

The following table shows the result of appeals against the decrees of each of the Subordinate Judicial Officers:[140]

The receipts and disbursement are shown below under the several heads :

Stamp Duty: The table given below shows the receipts under stamp duty for the last four years :[141]

1903 – 1904	Rs. 62,482
1904 – 1905	Rs. 70,376
1905 – 1906	Rs. 69,160
1906 – 1907	Rs. 70,133

The increase of Rs. 973 was mainly due to the institution of a big suit in the Court of the Civil judge.

II. Ameen's fees: Another table given below shows the receipts under the head of Ameen's fees for the last four year :[142]

1903 -1904	Rs. 702
1904 -1905	Rs. 783
1905 – 1906	Rs. 885
1906 – 1907	Rs. 804

III. Process of fees : The amount of Process –fees realized during the year was Rs. 19,930 against Rs. 20,255 of the previous year, showing a decrease of Rs. 325 only. The decrease was due to the decrease in the institutions.[143]

IV. Fines and forfeitures : These amounted to Rs. 233 against Rs. 553 of the previous year, showing a decrease of Rs. 320.[144]

Other receipts including copying fees : These amounted to Rs. 3,521 against Rs. 3,421 of the previous year, showing an increase of Rs. 100 only.[145]

The total receipts under the above heads were Rs. 94,621 against Rs. 94,273 of the previous year, showing an increase of Rs. 148 only.

Disbursement :[146]

Salary —— The Salary of judicial Officers amounted to Rs. 19,285 against Rs. 19,349 of the previous year, showing a decrease of Rs. 64 only.

Establishment charges ———— Amounted to Rs. 16,214 against Rs. 15,012 of the previous year showing an increase of Rs. 1202 only. This was mainly due to bonus and grain compensation allowance granted to certain officers.

Process –Service ——— The expenditure under this head was Rs. 9,286 against Rs. 8,008 of the previous year, showing an increase off Rs. 1,278 only. This was due to bonus and gain compensation allowed to the serving officers.

Contingencies ——— Amounted to Rs. 4,466 against Rs. 4,613 of the previous year, showing a decrease of Rs. 147 only.

Ameen's establishment ——— The cost of the establishment of the Civil Court Ameen was Rs. 864 against Rs. 875 of the previous year.

Unforeseen ———— The expenditure under this head amounted to Rs. 449 – 6 – 5 against Rs. 12 – 2 of the previous year.

The total amount of expenditure was Rs. 50,566 against Rs. 47,869 of the previous year, showing an increase of Rs. 2,697.

The net receipt of the Civil Department amounted to Rs. 44,055 against Rs. 46,404 of the previous year, showing a decrease of Rs. 2,349.

The total amount of fees realized during the year was Rs. 2,810 – 8 against Rs. 2,879 – 6, showing a decrease

Name of Courts	No. of copyrights	No. of comparing clerks	Average monthly income of each copyright	Remarks
			Rs. A. P.	
Sudder ---------	3	1	15 8 6	
		(a)		(a) The work was carried on by the regular staff
Toofangunj -------	1	-------	6 12 2	
Dinhata -----------	2	1	11 14 0	
Mathabhanga ----	2	1 (a)	12 14 0	
Mekhligunj --------	2	-------	• 11 0	

During the year under report, a record of 12,891 cases were received in the Record – Room as shown below :[148]

Courts	*Civil*	*Rent*	*Total*
Civil Judge Court	360	70	413
Assistant Civil Judge's Court	766	172	1,142
Sudder Rent Suit Court	——	1,199	1,435
Toofangunj	803	699	2,068
Dinhata	1,324	2,647	3,155
Mathabhanga	833	1,290	1,558
Mekhligunj	1,042	1,687	3,393
Total	5,128	7,763	12,891

The following records were destroyed during the year under report :[149]

Civil Judge's Court

Sudder ———————— B Files of Civil and Rent Original suits, Appeals, Miscellaneous and Execution cases from January to December 1896.

Assistant Civil Judge's Court

Sudder ———————— B Files of Civil and rent Original, Miscellaneous and Execution cases from January to December 1896.

Sudder ———————— Records of Small Cause Court Original, Miscellaneous and Execution cases from January 1896 to December 1898.

Sudder Sub Naib Ahilkar's Court

Sudder ———————— B Files of Civil and Rent Original suits from January to December 1896.

Toofangunj ———————— B Files of Civil and Rent Original suits and Execution cases from January to December 1896.

Naib Ahilkar's Court

Dinhata ———————— B Files of Civil and Rent Original suits, Miscellaneous and execution cases from January to December 1896.

Sub – Naib Ahilkar's Court

Dinhata ———————— B Files of Civil and Rent Original suits, Miscellaneous and Execution cases from January to December 1896.

Naib Ahilkar's Court

Mathabhanga ———————— B Files of Civil Execution and Miscellaneous cases and Rent Miscellaneous cases from January to December 1896.

Sub – Naib Ahilkar's Court

Mathabhanga ———————— B Files of Civil Original, Miscellaneous and Execution cases and Rent Miscellaneous and Execution cases from January to December 1896.

Mekhligunj ———————— B Files of Civil Miscellaneous and Execution cases and Rent Original, Miscellaneous and Execution cases from January to December 1896.

Mekhligunj ———————— Records of small Cause Court Original, Miscellaneous and Execution cases from January to December 1896.

In 1908 the Cooch Behar State Council held 31 meetings on its Judicial side against 25 of the previous year. The following table shows a graphic picture of work done by the State Council on its judicial side :[150]

Natures of cases	Pending at the beginning of the year	Installed during the year	Total	DISPOSED OF									Pending at the close of the year
				Received	Modified	Confiscated	Struck off	Remanded	Compromised	Rejected	Granted	Total	
CIVIL													
Regular appeals	1	4	5	1	1	1	-----	-----	1	-----	----	4	1
Special appeals	2	6	8	3	---	4	-----	----	-----	-----	-----	7	1
Miscellaneous	-----	1	1	1	----	----	-----	-----	-----	-----	----	1	-----
appeals													
Motions, etc.	1	------	1	1	-----	-----	----	-----	----	----	-----	1	-----
Miscellaneous	6	3	9	-----	----	-----	----	----	-----	8	1	9	-----
cases	-----	1	1	----	----	----	-----	-----	------	1	----	1	-----
Small Cause Court	-----	1	1	----	----	-----	-----	-----	------	-----	1	1	----
Reference													
RENT													
Special appeals	------	2	2	1	----	1	------	-----	----	-----	-----	2	-----
REVENUE		2	3	----	----	-----	-----	----	-----	1	1	2	1
Motions, etc.													
CRIMINAL													
Appeals	1	2											
Motions													
	----	8	8	-----	1	-----	------	-----	-----	7	----	8	------
	3	18	21	----	----	-----	1	------	----	15	5	21	-----
TOTAL	14	46	60	7	2	6	1	----	1	32	8	57	3

It will be seen that the number of cases pending at the close of the year was three only. On the legislative and executive side, 43 meetings were held against 33 of the previous year at 18 of which Maharaja presided. The Cooch Behar Penal Code and an Act to amend the Cooch Behar Stamp Act I of 1903 were passed into law during the year of report.[151]

In 1909 the Council held 26 meetings on its Judicial side against 31 of the previous year. At two of these meetings Maharaja presided and heard a criminal appeal against an order of the Session Judge of the state acquitting an accused person of the charge of murder under section 302 of the Indian Penal code and the Rules of Cooch Behar. The appeal was presented by the Public Prosecutor under Section 417 of the Criminal Procedure Code. The following table shows the work done by the State Council on its judicial side :[152] (see table on facing page).

Cooch Behar Act I of 1909, being the Code of Criminal Procedure was passed into law during the year of report, and two Bills, (1) An Act for the Registration of Births and Deaths in Municipal towns and (2) the Cooch Behar Tenancy Bill are under consideration of the Legislative Council. The Code of Criminal Procedure based on the law in force in British India, with some slight modifications to suit the special circumstances of the State. The Cooch Behar Tenancy Bill is a very important measure as it deals with the rights of landlords and tenants; it has been framed after a good deal of consideration and discussion.[153]

The following table of 1910 shows the change of officers in the Subordinate Judicial Courts :[154]

Sub Divisions	*Names of officers*	*Terms of employment*
Sudder	Harendra Narayan Chowdhuri, B.L.Offg. Assistant Civil Judge	From the 1st April 1909 to the 3rd of February 1910.
Sudder	Gopal Chandra Chatterjee,	From the 7th February to the

Natures of cases	Pending at the beginning of the year	Installed during the year	Total	DISPOSED OF									Pending at the close of the year
				Received	Modified	Confirmed	Remanded	Compromised	Rejected	Granted	Remarks	Total	
CIVIL													
Regular appeals	1	1	2	1	----	-----	-----	1	----	-----	----	2	-----
Special appeals	1	15	16	2	---	12	-----	1	-----	-----	-----	15	1
Miscellaneous appeals	-----	1	1	----	----	----	-----	-----	-----	-----	----	-----	1
Motions, etc.	-----	5	5	----	-----	-----	2	-----	3	----	-----	5	-----
Miscellaneous	-----	2	2	-----	----	-----	----	-----	1	-----	----	1	1
cases	-----	2	2	----	----	----	-----	-----	------	----	----	2	-----
Small Cause Court												5	----
Reference													
RENT	------	4	5	----	----	2	1	-----	3	-----	----		
Special appeals	1	1	1	----	----	1	------	-----	----	-----	-----	1	-----
REVENUE												3	1
Motions, etc.	----	3	3	----	----	1	-----	----	2	----	----		
CRIMINAL													
Appeals	----												
Motions	------	4	4	-----	---	1	------	-----	2	1	----	3	------
													1
TOTAL	3	38	41	3	----	17	3	2	11	1	----	37	4

B.L., Assistant Civil Judge 31st of March 1910.

Sudder Rai Choudhuri Satish From 1st of April 1909 to the
31st Chandra Mustafi, Sudder
of March 1910 Rent Suit Naib
Ahilkar

Sudder Jatindra Mohan Sen Gupta, From the 16th of June to the
16th B.L., Peripatetic Sub
of July 1909. Naib Ahilkar

Toofangunj Narasinha Chandra Ghosh, From the 1st April to the 21st of
M.A., B.L., Sub Naib July 1909 and from the 2nd of
Ahilkar November 1909 to the 31st of
March 1910.

Toofangunj Jotindra Mohan Sen Gupta, From the 2nd July to the 1st of
B.L., Offg., Naib Ahilkar November 1909.

Dinhata Pramath Nath Chatterjee, From the 1st April to the 20th
M.A., B.L., Naib Ahilkar November1909 and from the
20th January to the 31st of March
1910.

Dinhata Jotindra Mohan Sen Gupta, From 21st November 1909 to
the B.L., Offg., Naib Ahilkar
19th of January 1910

Mathabhnaga Ashutosh Ghosh, B.L., From the 1st of April 1909 to
the Naib Ahilkar 31st of
March 1910.

Mathabhanga Jotindra Mohan Sen Gupta, From the 8th of April to the 1st
of B.L., Offg., Naib Ahilkar
June 1909 and from the 26th of January to the 31st
of March 1910.

Mekhligunj Hari Nath Basu, B.L., From the 1st of April 1909 to
the Naib Ahilkar 31st of
March 1910.

The original suits instituted during the last four years are shown below :[155]

Years	*Civil suits*	*Rent suits*	*Small cause Court suits up to Rs. 50 and Rs. 20*	*Total*
1906 – 07	1,689	3,269	1,617	6,575
1907 – 08	2,027	3,200	1,541	6,768
1908 – 09	1,338	3,467	2,121	6,926

1909 – 10	1,467	3,666	2,170	7,303

It will appear from the above that the number of institutions during the year under report was 7,303 against 6,926 of the previous year, showing an increase of 377 suits.

The table given below shows the increase and decrease in the institutions in the several Civil and Rent Courts of the State :[156]

Courts	*Civil Suits*		*Rent Suits*	
	Increase	*Decrease*	*Increase*	*Decrease*
Civil Judge	7	—	—	1
Assistant Civil Judge	—	42	107	—
Sudder Rent Suit Officer	—	—	2	—
Naib Ahilkar, Toofangunj	129	—	11	—
Naib Ahilkar, Dinhata	51	18	82	—
Naib Ahilkar, Mathabhanga	71	—	—	7
Sub Naib Ahilkar Mathabhanga	5	—	1	—
Naib Ahilkar, Mekhligunj	—	38	4	—
Total	258	80	207	8

Civil suits increased in the Courts of the Civil Judge and the Naib Ahilkars of Toofangunj, Dinhata, Mathabhanga and the Sub Naib Ahilkar of Mathabhanga by 2,129, 51, 71, 5, respectively and decreased in the Courts of the Assistant Civil Judge and the Naib Ahilkar of Mekhligunj by 42 and 38 respectively. Rent suits increased in the Courts of the Assistant Civil Judge, Sudder Rent Suit Naib Ahilkar, The Naib Ahilkar of Toofangunj, Dinhata, Mekhligunj and the Sub Naib Ahilkar of Mathabhanga by 107, 2, 11, 82, 4, and 1 respectively and decreased in the Courts of the Civil Judge and the Naib Ahilkar of Mathabhnaga by 1 and 7 respectively.[157]

The increase of institutions is too slight to call for remarks.

Statement No. 2 shows that out of a total of 7,303 institutions, 3164 were suits on bonds and other obligations 3,666 were rent suits, 463 for land and other immovable properties and 10 relating to matrimonial rights.

The number of applications for execution of decrees during the last four years is shown in the table given below :[158]

Years	*Civil*	*Rent*	*Small cause*	*Total Court suits*
1906 – 07	1,333	1,436	635	3,404
1907 – 08	1,499	1,362	682	3,543
1908 – 09	1,421	1,296	853	3,570
1909 – 10	1,319	1,267	873	3,159

The number of applications filed during the year under review was 3,459 against 3,570 of the previous year, showing a decrease of 111 applications.

The number of miscellaneous cases instituted during the last two years is shown below :[159]

Year	*Judicial*	*Non-Judicial*
1908–09	408	40
1909–10	523	39

The number of applications for certificates of guardianship under Act VI of 1897 was 81 against 71 of the previous year, showing an increase of 10 applications and the number of applications for certificates under Act V of 1898 was 60 against 55 of the previous year showing an increase of 5 applications.

The number of applications filed under the probate and Administration Act was 18 against 12 of the previous year and the number disposed of was 16 against 19 of the previous year.

According to the number of original suits instituted the subordinate courts rank thus :[160]

- Assistant Civil Judge ———— 2088
- Naib Ahilkar, Mathabhanga ———— 1811
- Naib Ahilkar, Dinhata ———— 1737
- Naib Ahilkar, Mekhligunj ———— 921

- Naib Ahilkar, Tufangunj ———————— 715

The disposal of original suits during the last four years is shown in the statement given below :[161]

Years	Civil	Rent Court suits	Small cause	Total
1906 – 07	1,598	3,287	1,610	6,495
1907 – 08	1,968	3,162	1,534	6,644
1908 – 09	1,336	3,419	2,169	6,924
1909 – 10	1,500	3,709	2,147	7,356

The total number of original suits disposed of was 7,356 against 6,924 of the previous year showing an increase of 432 suits.

According to disposals the subordinate courts rank thus :[162]

- Assistant Civil Judge ———————— 1781
- Naib Ahilkar, Dinhata ———————— 1709
- Naib Ahilkar, Mathabhanga ———————— 1422
- Naib Ahilkar, Mekhligunj ———————— 936
- Naib Ahilkar, Tufangunj ———————— 692
- Peripatetic Sub Naib Ahilkar ———————— 531
- Sudder Rent Suit Naib Ahilkar ———————— 263

The following table compares the number of contested original suits for last four years :[163]

Years	Civil	Rent	Small cause Court suits	Total
1906 – 07	451	399	254	1,104
1907 – 08	532	358	265	1,155
1908 – 09	486	409	332	1,227
1909 – 10	525	445	349	1,319

The total number of contested suits decided was 1319 being less than one-fifth of the entire number of disposals.

With regard to the disposal of contested suits, the subordinate courts rank thus :[164]

- Naib Ahilkar, Mathabhanga —————— 303
- Assistant Civil Judge —————— 301

Name of Courts	Civil Suits				Rent Suits				Small cases Court suits			
	Contested		Uncontested		Contested		Uncontested		Contested		Uncontested	
	m.	d.	m.	d.	m.	d.	m.	d.	m.	d.	m.	d.
Assistant Civil Judge	9	17	5	19	3	17	0	29	1	13	1	2
Sudder Rent Suit Courts	4	10	——				0	27	——		——	
Toofangunj Court	4	10	1	9	2	13	0	23	1	10	0	29
Dinhata Court	4	15	1	5	0	27	1		1		0	22
Mathabhanga Court	5	23	1		3	28	22		8		1	5
	3	20			3	0						
Mekhligunj Court			17		2	7	1	4	2		1	5
			1	7			0		3			
							28		2			
									14			

The duration was longest in the Court of the Assistant Civil Judge and shortest in that of Tufangunj.

Out of the total number of original suits disposed of 2,089 or less than one –third were for claims not exceeding Rs. 20; 2,589 or more than one-third were for claims exceeding Rs. 20 but not exceeding Rs. 50; 1,515 or less than one-fifth were for claims exceeding Rs. 50 but not exceeding Rs. 100; 1,100 or less than one-sixth were for claims exceeding Rs. 100 but not Rs. 500; 41 were for claims exceeding Rs. 500 but not exceeding Rs. 1000. There were 20 suits exceeding Rs. 1,000 but not exceeding Rs. 5,000. There was one suit exceeding Rs. 5,000 but not exceeding Rs. 10,000 and one exceeding Rs. 10,000 but not exceeding Rs. 1,00,000.[166]

The number of old suits pending at the close of the year was 23 (19 pending over six months and 4 pending over one year) against 76 of the previous year.

All Naib Ahilkars with the exception of the Naib Ahilkar of Tufangunj tried Small Cause Court Suits up to Rs. 100 adopting summary procedure.

The statement given below shows the disposal of execution cases during the last four years :[167]

Years	*Civil*	*Rent*	*Small cause Court suits upto Rs. 50 and Rs. 20*	*Total*
1906 – 07	1,371	1,460	651	3,482
1907 – 08	1,456	1,323	667	3,446
1908 – 09	1,457	1,303	829	3,589
1909 – 10	1,305	1,300	851	3,456

The total number of Execution cases disposed of was 3,456 against 3,589 of the previous year showing a decrease of 133 cases.

The table given below shows the disposal of miscellaneous cases :[168]

	Judicial	*Non Judicial*
Civil	321	41
Rent	131	—
Small Cause Court up to Rs. 100 and Rs. 20	75	—
Total	527	41

The number of cases made over to the Civil Court Amin for local enquiry by the Civil Courts of the State was 129 against 134 of the previous year. One case remained pending enquiry at the close of the year.

The statement given below shows the work of the Civil Judge's Court on the civil side for the last three years :[169] (see table on facing page)

Sixteen Original, 16 Execution and 53 Miscellaneous cases were pending at the close of the year.

The following table shows the total number of Regular

Years	Original Suits				Execution				Miscellaneous			
	Pending from last year	Instituted or received by transfer	Disposed of	Pending	Pending from last year	Instituted or received by transfer	Disposed of	Pending	Pending from last year	Instituted or received transfer	Disposed of	Pending
1907 – 08	19	15	21	13	8	28	29	7	23	161	124	60
1908 – 09	13	21	17	17	7	32	32	7	60	142	166	36
1909 - 10	16	22	22	16	7	29	20	16	36	170	153	53

and Miscellaneous appeals preferred in the Civil Judge's Court during the last three years :[170]

1907 – 08 ———— 142

1908 – 09 ———— 144

1909 – 1910 ———— 146

The number of appeals filed during the year under report was 146 against 144 of the previous year showing an increase of 2 appeals.

The result of appeals for the last three years is shown in the table given below :[171]

Year	*No. of appeals for disposed*	*Confirmed*	*Reversed*	*Modified*	*Disposed of otherwise*	*Pending*
1907 – 1908	201	102	23	8	2	66

Name of Officers	Details of Disposals						Total disposed of	Remarks
	Confirmed	Reversed	Modified	Remanded	Disposed on default	Compromised		
Raj Krishna Das, L.C.E.	----	------	---	-----	-----	1	1	
Harendra Narayan Choudhury, B.L.	23	8	2	1	----	------	34	
Ashutosh Ghosh, B.L.	15	4	4	------	------	----	23	
Hari Nath Basu, B.L.	13	5	2	-----	----	1	21	
Pramatha Nath Chatterjee, M.A.,B.L.	21	11	2	------	----	-----	34	
Narasinha Chandra Ghosh, M.A., B.L	10	2	1	------	----	----	13	
Jotindra Mohan Sen Gupta, B.L.	10	4	1	-----	----	------	15	
Total	92	34	12	1	---	2	141	

The receipts and disbursements are shown below under several heads :

***Receipts* :**[174]

Stamp Duty ——————————— The table given below shows the receipts under this head for the last four years :

	Rs.
1906 – 07	70,133
1907 – 08	72,168
1908 – 09	75,883
1909 – 10	90,661

The increase of Rs. 14778 was mainly due to the institution of a big suit in the Civil Judge's Court towards the end of the year under report and to the increase in the number of institutions.

Amin's Fees ——————— The table given below shows the receipts under this head for the last four years:

	Rs.
1906 – 07	804
1907 – 08	1,035
1908 – 09	963
1909 – 10	924

Process Fees ————— The amount of process fees 7c., realized during the year under report was Rs.21,709 against Rs.21,029 of the previous year, showing an increase of Rs. 761 only. The increase was in respect of sale-fees.

Fines and forfeitures ——————These amounted to Rs. 188 against Rs. 105 of the previous year, showing an increase of Rs. 83.

Other receipts including copying fees ———These amounted to Rs. 4,184 against Rs. 3,587 of the previous year, showing an increase of Rs. 597. The increase was due to larger institutions of suits.

The total receipts under the above heads were Rs. 1,17,747 against Rs. 1,01,567 of the previous year, showing an increase of Rs. 16,180. The causes of increase have been noted under each head.

Disbursements :[175]

Salary ———————— The salary of judicial officers amounted to Rs.18,053 against Rs. 17, 481 of the previous year showing an increase of Rs. 572. The increase was mainly due to the appointment of a Peripatetic Sub Naib Ahilkar.

Establishment charges ———— Amounted to Rs. 17,987 against Rs. 16,288 of the previous year, showing an increase of Rs. 1,699. This was due to the increment of pay sanctioned by Maharaja on the recommendation of the salary Committee.

Process service ———— The expenditure under this head was Rs. 9,797 against Rs. 9,554 of the previous year showing an increase of Rs. 243 only.

Contingencies ———— Amounted to Rs. 4,967 against Rs. 6,138 of the previous year, showing a decrease of Rs. 1,171. The decrease is apparent only, in as much as the figure for 1908 – 09 included Rs. 1,200 for "Horse Allowance".

Amin's Establishment ——— The cost of establishment of the Civil Court Amin was Rs. 964 against Rs. 895 of the previous year, showing an increase of Rs. 69 only.

Unforeseen ———— The expenditure under this head amounted to Rs. 102 against Rs. 480 of the previous year, showing a decrease of Rs. 378.

The total amount of expenditure was Rs. 51,870 against Rs. 50,837 of the previous year, showing an increase of Rs. 1,033 only.

The net receipt of the Civil Department amounted to Rs. 65,877 against Rs.50,730 of the previous year, showing

Name of Courts	No. of copyrights	No. of comparing clerks	Average monthly income of each copyright	Remarks
			Rs. A. P.	
Sudder ----------	3	1 (a)	22 10 3	(a) The work was carried on by the regular staff
Toofangunj --------	1	--------	8 10 4	
Dinhata -----------	2	1	14 14 4	
Mathabhanga -----	2	1 (a)	16 10 0	
Mekhligunj --------	3	--------	8 13 11	

During the year under report, a record of 7,334 cases were received in the Record – Room as shown below :[177]

Courts	*Civil*	*Rent*	*Total*
Civil Judge Court	503	52	555
Assistant Civil Judge's Court	1568	1,143	1,568
Dinhata	735	1241	1,878
Mathabhanga	979	708	2,220
Mekhligunj	405	1290	1113
Total	4190	3144	7334

The following records were destroyed during the year under report :[178]

Civil Judge's Court

Sudder —————— B Files of Civil and Rent Original suits, Appeals, Miscellaneous and Execution cases from January to December 1899.

Assistant Civil Judge's Court

Sudder——————————B Files of Civil and rent Original, Miscellaneous and Execution cases from January to December 1899.

Rent Suit Naib Ahilkar

Sudder——————————B Files of Rent Original suits, Miscellaneous and Execution cases from January to December 1899.

Toofangunj——————————B Files of Civil and Rent Original suits and Execution cases from January to December 1899.

Naib Ahilkar's Court

Dinhata——————————B Files of Civil and Rent Original suits, Miscellaneous and execution cases from January to December 1899.

Sub – Naib Ahilkar's Court

Dinhata——————————B Files of Civil and Rent Original suits, Miscellaneous and Execution cases from January to December 1899.

Naib Ahilkar's Court

Mathabhanga——————————B Files of Civil Execution and Miscellaneous cases and Rent Miscellaneous cases from January to December 1899.

Sub – Naib Ahilkar's Court

Mathabhanga——————————B Files of Civil Original, Miscellaneous and Execution cases and Rent Miscellaneous and Execution cases from January to December 1899.

Mekhligunj——————————B Files of Civil Miscellaneous and Execution cases and Rent Original, Miscellaneous and Execution cases from January to December 1899.

From the above analysis it can be said that during the reign of Maharaja Nripendra Narayan all sorts of initiatives were taken in this field, which gave a line of systematic work for the upcoming years. Such an arrangement on the whole was truly a remarkable initiative so far as activities were concern. The ruling authority on this very point proved the modern outlook of the administrative work of the State.

NOTES AND REFERENCES

1. Annual Administration Report of the Cooch Behar State (1878-79), p. 26.
2. *Ibid*.

3. *Ibid.*, p. 27.
4. *Ibid.*
5. *Ibid.*
6. *Ibid.*
7. *Ibid.*, p. 28.
8. *Ibid.*
9. *Ibid.*
10. *Ibid.*, p.29.
11. *Ibid.*
12. *Ibid.*
13. *Ibid.*
14. *Ibid.*, p. 30.
15. Annual Administration Report of the Cooch Behar State (1880-81), p. 19.
16. *Ibid.*, p. 20.
17. *Ibid.*
18. *Ibid.*, p. 21.
19. *Ibid.*
20. *Ibid.*
21. *Ibid.*, p. 22.
22. *Ibid.*
23. *Ibid.*, p. 23.
24. *Ibid.*
25. *Ibid.*, p. 24.
26. Annual Administration Report of the Cooch Behar State (1882-83), p. 26.
27. *Ibid.*, p. 27.
28. *Ibid.*
29. *Ibid.*
30. *Ibid.*
31. *Ibid.*, p. 28.
32. *Ibid.*, p. 29.
33. *Ibid.*
34. *Ibid.*, p. 30.

35. *Ibid.*
36. *Ibid.* p. 31.
37. Annual Administration Report of the Cooch Behar State (1885-86), 2.
38. *Ibid.*
39. *Ibid.*
40. *Ibid.*
41. *Ibid.*, p. 3.
42. *Ibid.*
43. *Ibid.*
44. *Ibid.*, p. 4.
45. *Ibid.*
46. *Ibid.*
47. Annual Administration Report of the Cooch Behar State (1888-89), p. 4.
48. *Ibid.*
49. Annual Administration Report of the Cooch Behar State (1889-90), p. 2.
50. *Ibid.*
51. *Ibid.*, p. 4.
52. Annual Administration Report of the Cooch Behar State (1898-99), p. 3.
53. Annual Administration Report of the Cooch Behar State (1900 – 01), p. 3.
54. *Ibid.*
55. *Ibid.*
56. *Ibid.*
57. *Ibid.*, p. 4.
58. Annual Administration Report of the Cooch Behar State (1901- 02), p. 2.
59. *Ibid.*
60. *Ibid.*
61. *Ibid.*
62. *Ibid.*, p. 3.
63. *Ibid.*

64. *Ibid*.
65. *Ibid*.
66. *Ibid*.
67. *Ibid*., p. 4.
68. *Ibid*.
69. *Ibid*.
70. *Ibid*.
71. *Ibid*.
72. *Ibid*., p. 5.
73. *Ibid*.
74. *Ibid*.
75. *Ibid*., p. 6.
76. *Ibid*.
77. *Ibid*., p. 7.
78. *Ibid*.
79. *Ibid*.
80. *Ibid*.
81. *Ibid*.
82. *Ibid*.
83. *Ibid*.
84. *Ibid*.
85. *Ibid*., p. 8.
86. *Ibid*.
87. *Ibid*.
88. *Ibid*.
89. Annual Administration Report of the Cooch Behar State (1902 - 1903), p. 2.
90. *Ibid*.
91. *Ibid*.
92. *Ibid*.
93. *Ibid*.
94. *Ibid*., p. 3.
95. *Ibid*.
96. *Ibid*.

97. *Ibid*.
98. *Ibid*.
99. *Ibid*., p. 4.
100. *Ibid*.
101. *Ibid*.
102. *Ibid*., p. 5.
103. *Ibid*.
104. *Ibid*.
105. *Ibid*.
106. *Ibid*., p. 6.
107. *Ibid*.
108. *Ibid*.
109. *Ibid*.
110. *Ibid*., p. 7.
111. *Ibid*.
112. *Ibid*., p. 8.
113. *Ibid*.
114. *Ibid*.
115. *Ibid*.
116. *Ibid*.
117. *Ibid*.
118. *Ibid*., p. 9.
119. *Ibid*.
120. *Ibid*., p. 10.
121. *Ibid*.
122. Annual Administration Report of the Cooch Behar State (1904 – 05), p. 1.
123. *Ibid*., p. 2.
124. Annual Administration Report of the Cooch Behar State (1906 – 07), p. 1.
125. *Ibid*.
126. *Ibid*.
127. *Ibid*.
128. *Ibid*.

129. *Ibid.*, p. 2.
130. *Ibid.*
131. *Ibid.*
132. *Ibid.*
133. *Ibid.*
134. *Ibid.*, p. 3.
135. *Ibid.*
136. *Ibid.*
137. *Ibid.*
138. *Ibid.*, p. 4.
139. *Ibid.*
140. *Ibid.*, p. 5.
141. *Ibid.*
142. *Ibid.*, p. 6.
143. *Ibid.*
144. *Ibid.*, p. 7.
145. *Ibid.*
146. *Ibid.*, p. 8.
147. *Ibid.*
148. *Ibid.*, p. 9
149. *Ibid.*
150. Annual Administration Report of the Cooch Behar State (1907 – 08), p. 1.
151. *Ibid.*, p. 2.
152. Annual Administration Report of the Cooch Behar State (1908 – 09), p. 1.
153. *Ibid.*, p. 2.
154. Annual Administration Report of the Cooch Behar State (1909 – 10), p. 1.
154. *Ibid.*, p. 2.
155. *Ibid.*
156. *Ibid.*
157. *Ibid.*, p. 3.
158. *Ibid.*
159. *Ibid.*

160. *Ibid*.
161. *Ibid*.
162. *Ibid*.
163. *Ibid*., p. 4.
164. *Ibid*.
165. *Ibid*.
166. *Ibid*.
167. *Ibid*., p. 5.
168. *Ibid*.
169. *Ibid*.
170. *Ibid*.
171. *Ibid*., p. 6.
172. *Ibid*.
173. *Ibid*.
174. *Ibid*., p. 7.
175. *Ibid*.
176. *Ibid*., p. 8.
177. *Ibid*., p. 9.
178. *Ibid*.

2

Department of Criminal Justice in Cooch Behar State

The State of Cooch Behar represents a technical sounded field in the administrative measures. The administration of criminal justice is not an exception to that. During the monarchical period the State saw the implementation of various kinds of steps in order to move the administration of the monarchy. Specially during the rule of Maharaja Nripendra Narayan, known as the modernizer of the State initiated important measures in this department. An attempt has been made in the present chapter to discuss in detail manner the administration of justice in criminal cases and along with this a chronological data has been incorporated in this matter so far as records are concern. Here it can be include that Maharaja ushered an era of modernity in every sphere when he attained maturity i.e. in 1878. The administration formed a constructive framework under the guidance of the Maharaja, who gave it a new term, character and meaning.. Let us now discuss in detail the judicial system of the State during those days .

In 1878 -79, the Charge of the Chief Criminal Court of original jurisdiction rested with Fouzdari Ahilkar, throughout the year. The total number of cases of all description reported during the year was 2,993 cases 1,577 were cognizable and 1,416 were non – cognizable cases have therefore increased by 6 and non – cognizable cases by 95. Among the cognizable cases, the serious offences against the person were 84 against 107 and serious offences against property were 35 against 42 of the previous year.[1] The prevailing crimes, as in other years, have been petty thefts, trespass and assaults. Under the head of petty theft there is a decrease in the number reported, contrary to my expectations, the total being 936 against 983 of the previous year and of the actual cases reported no less than 156 were ascertained to be fales, leaving a total of 780 true cases against 838 of the previous year. There is an increase of 31 cases of assault, the number being 522 against 491 of the previous year.[2]

Comparative statement of all Courts ——— The subjoined statement shews the number of cases reported and the number of persons brought to trial in all Courts in the past and preceding years:[3]

Details.	*1877 – 78*	*1878 -79*
Number of Cognizable and Non- cognizable cases reported	2,892	2,993
Number of persons brought to trial ———	1,921	1,884
Convicted ———	1316	1,221
Released ———	558	635
Otherwise disposed of ———	19	9
Remaining under trial at the end of the year ——	28	19
Percentage of persons convicted total number brought to tria	70.2	95.75

A decrease of 37 is observed in the number of persons brought to trial; 169 petty theft cases were not enquired into under Section 117 of the Procedure Code and summonses were refused in 323 frivolous and false cases instituted directly before Magisterial officers. The percentage of persons convicted is a little lower than that of the preceding year in as much as it has decreased from 70.2 to 65.78.

The table given below gives additional details for the

past year, showing the number of persons brought to trial in all Courts in Cognizable and Non-cognizable Crime returns herewith submitted:[4]

Details	*Cognizable*	*Non-Cognizable*
Cases reported	1,577	1,416
Number of Persons under trial	912(a)	972(f)
Convicted	601(b)	629(g)
Released	296(c)	839(h)
Otherwise disposed of	5(d)	4(i)
Remaining under trial at the end of the year—	10(e)	9(j)
Percentage of persons convicted total number tried	67.001	64.6

Column XV. a	Column XI. F
Column III., b	Column XV, XVI. G
Column XVII. C	Column XII, XIII, XIV., h
Column XIX. D	Column XVIII. I
Column XXII, XXIII. E	Column XVII. J

It will be observed that the proportion of convictions in both cognizeble and Non- cognizable cases is lower than in the previous year, there being only 19 cases under tried and 2 appeals undisposed of.

There were 35 criminal appeals during the year against 30 of the previous year. In 15 cases the order of the lower court were confirmed in 10 cases modified and in 7 reversed. The table given below shows the numberof persons convicted and of appeals preferred with the result in the case of each officer separately.[5]

Name of officers against whose decisions appeals were prefered	Total number of persons punished	Total number of appeals	Order confirmed	Order modified	Order reversed	pending
Babu Bodhesh Chunder Chakroberty, Foujdari Ahilkar	277	15	5	6	3	1
Babu Hari Das Majumdar, offg, Naib Ahilkar	88	7	5	2	-----	——
Kumar Keshav Narayan, Assistant Ahilkar	312	7	3	------	2	2
Babu Peary Lal Roy, Naib Ahilkar	83	1	-----	------	1	——
Babu Bhuvan Halder, Naib Ahilkar	155	2	1	1	——	——
Babu Kedar Nath Mukherjee, Naib Ahilkar	151	......	------	------	——	-------
Kumar Rangalal Narayan, Naib Ahilkar	145	3	1	1	1	——
TOTAL	1,211	35	15	10	7	3

The Deputy Commissioner heard 22 and the Fauzdari Ahilkar 13 cases. Two cases only of murder were reported during the year, of these one was a case of murder and suicide. Inspection of records of the case and an compelled to agree with the Fauzdari Ahilkar that the evidence would not supported conviction; but from the coincidence of the time of the woman's disappearance witht that fixed for the trial of the maintenance, cases, there seems to strongest ground for suspecting Brojo Dass of having made away with him and have directed the case to be made over to an intelligent officer with a via of eliciting any evidence that may not hitherto have come to light.[6] One case of murder which occurred before the commencement of year under report was under investigation during the year, but the suspect, arderer being a foreigner and having left the State; it was found impossible to him.

There were 6 cases of culpable homicide reported during the year against one in the previous year. Of these one was declared false; in two cases the reasons accused were found to be protected by the right of private defence and were discharged under section 103 I.P.C. In the forth case the accused was sentenced five years rigorous imprisonment. In the fifth case there was possibly a failure justice. The accused was charged with having strangled his girl wife and thrown her into the river. The case was reported at first as one of drowning but subsequently suspicion fell on the husband and the Police taking the matter up and arresting him, he made as alleged a full confession of having killed his wife and was immediately taken before the Naib Ahilkar to whom he repeated his state attend before the Police.[7] The Naib Ahilkar however contented himself with simply recording the confession and failed to examine a single witness, although severed are brought before him at the time, pleading as his excuse when called upon to explain that he did not like to examine witnesses fresh from the Police. The supiriority of the excuse was manifest, as he had not hesitated to record the confession which was to say the least as likely to be due to Police influence any thing the witness might say.[8] When subsequently examined the witnesses told quite a different story and the accused retracted his confession, stating cases told quite a different story and the accused retracted his confession, stating amount he had been forced into making it.[9] From the circumstances of the case and from the fact that prior to the Police investigation the case had been reported at the as a case of drowning and that the members of the family had their story due or otherwise of the way the accident occurred ready before the Police took up the enquary, as was proved by the report of the information entered at the thana, it seemed exceedingly improbable that these very relatives and the accused husband with whome they had sided, would have told quite a different story, inculpating the husband, unless were not examined at the time the confession was recorded and as they adhered, when examined afterwards, to the story which had first been given at thana, it was impossible to convict the prisoner simply on his confession when fresh from Police custody, which he retracted subsequently both before the Naib Ahilkar and self. Whether the confession was true or not cannot decide, it was not altogether voluntary. The Naib Ahilkar severly both for his careless and sepcially enquiry and for his disingenuous excuses for it.[10]

There were three cases of dacoity reported during the year against three of the preceding year. These added to the two cases reported in the last year, but disposed of in the year under report, make the total number of cases five; of those one was found to be false and two are yet pending with the Police. In the two remaining cases the police had sent up 10 men for trial; of those six men were convicted and sentenced to 10 years regorous imprisonment each and four were released.[11]

One of the seven cases of rape reported during the year only two were sent up for trial, of these one resulted in the conviction of the accused and he was sentenced to five years regorous imprisonment. In the other case, a boy of some 17 to 18 years old was asserted to have committed rape upon a girl of three, but as medical examination showed that three was no rupture or any external marks of violence.[12]

The sub-joined table shows the distribution of work amongst the several officers :[13]

Name of Officers	No. of cases	No. of persons under trial	Convicted	Acquited or discharged	Otherwise disposed of	Remaining under trial at the end of the year	Percentage of persons convicted to total number tried
G.T.D alton, Esq., Deputy Commissioner	14	28	16	4	----------	8	80
Babu Jadab Chandra Chukroborty,	1,061	443	275	159	7	2	63.3
Fouzdari Ahilkar	125	174	88	86	---------	-----	50.5
Hari Das Mukherjee,Naib Ahilkar	120	143	82	58	---------	3	58.5
Peary lal Roy, Naib Ahilkar	310	449	310	138	1	------	69.1
Kumar Keshav Narayan , Assist Ahilkar	390	228	155	67	--------	6	69.8
Sashi Bhusan Haldar, Naib Ahilkar	553	197	151	45	1	-------	77.04
Kedar Nath mukherjee, Naib Ahilkar	420	222	144	78	-------	---------	64.8
Kumar Rangila Narayan, Naib Ahilkar							
Total	2,993	1,884	1,226	635	9	19	66.05

The Criminal Courts had occasion to take attachment proceedings against 8 defendants during the year. Rs. 117 were awarded as compensation to defendants, (Section 209 of Criminal Procedure Code). Proceedings had to be taken in 18 cases for the suppression of local nuisances under XXIX.

The Statement given below will show the result of fine operations in the past and in the preceeding years:[14]

Years	Balance of the previous year	Imposed during the year	Realized during the year	Remitted or written off	Balance at the end of the year
	Rs. A.	Rs. A.	Rs. A. P.	Rs. A.	Rs. A.
1877 - 78	P.	P.	6,317 2 2	P.	P.
1878 - 79	4,012 13 1	8,276 3 0	7,453 12 6	2,370 11 10	3,601 2 1
	3,601 2 1	9,125 8 0		2,285 3 2	2,987 10 5

It will appear that the balance which remained unrealized at the end of the year under report was Rs. 2,987 – 10 – 5 against Rs. 3,601 – 2 – 1 of the previous year. The fact that fines imposed upon very poor people who undergo alternative imprisonment in liue thereof have been ordered to be written off, accounts for the heavy sum that appears under the heading "written off or remitted."[15]

The assessment for the year under report was Rs.2,158 – 2; this amount added to Rs. 3-13-9, the realizable balance of the previous year, gives a total of Rs. 2,161 – 15 – 9 ; deducting from this amount the sum of Rs. 112-14-6 on account of persons who have died, left their places &C., there remain Rs. 2,048 – 14 -3; of these, Rs. 2,041 – 10 - 6 were realized, leaving a balance of Rs. 7-6-9. The result is generally satisfactory. The cost of the chowkidari establishment was Rs. 2,040 against Rs. 2,027 -13-3 of the previous year, showing an increase of Rs. 12-2-9.[16]

During the year 1881 - 82, the total number of cases of all descriptions reported was 2,132 aganst 2,399 of the preceeding year showing a decrease of 267 cases. Of these 1,034 were cognizable cause against 1,255 and 1,098 were non –cognizable aganst 1,144 of the previous year. Cognizable cases have, therefore, decreased by 221 and non –cognizable cause by 46. It is satisfactory to observe that crime has been steadily decreasing during the last two years, as will appear from the statement given below:[17]

YEAR	*OFFENCE*		*TOTAL*
	Cognizable	*Non-Cognizable*	
1878 – 79	1,577	1,416	2,903
1879 – 80	1,255	1,144	2,399
1880 - 81	1,034	1,098	2,132

Among the congnizable cases serious offences against the person were 74 against 60 and serious offences against property were 48 against 41 of the previous year. The number of petty thefts has come down from 730 to 537 in the year under report. It was 936 in the year 1877 -78. In the year 1878 -79 the total number of cases was 2,993. In the following year 1879 -80 this total fell to 2,399 and in the year under review the total has again fallen to 2,132. The decrease between 1878-79 and 1879-80 (594) was more than double that in the present year; the figure being 267. There are several causes at work to which this large decrease of crime is attributable, but the principal one is probably the great reduction in the price of food grains. This assumption is strengthened by the fact that (1) there was a very large reduction in the price of rice after the cutting of the 1879 harvest, that is, it fell by nearly one half and (2) there has been a further though much smaller reduction since the 1880 crop was harvested. The subject of the reduction of prices has already been dealt with in the Land Revenue Report.[18]

There has been only a slight decrease (10 only) in the number of assult cases. It was 459 in the previous year, but in the year under report, the number was 449. The prevailing crimes continue to be thefts and assults. There were three dacoity cases reported during the last year against none in the previous year, and the amount of property plundered has been mentioned to be Rs. 1,051 – 5 – 0. All these three dacoities were committed in the jurisdiction of the sub–division of Mekhligunj. In 1878 -79 a daring dacoity was committed in that Sub–division by a gang of 14 people of Gazipore. The case was sucessfully enquired into and the culprits severly punished by the Session Court. The opening of the North bengal State Railway has greatly facilitated the increase of these dacoities of the North Western Provinces in to the Raj, and the railway station of Haldibari, being situated in Mekhliguni, the dacoits committed their depredations in that Subdivision. It was aware of this hoped that the present state of things will no longer continue.[19]

The statement given below shows the number of cases reported and the number of persons brought to trial in all courts in the past and preceding years :[20]

PARTICULAR	*1879-80*	*1880-81*
Number of Cognizable and Non–Cognizable cases reported	2300	2,122
Number of persons brought to trial	1879	1,818
Convicted	1173	1,196
Released	668	590
Otherwise disposed of	1	15
Remaining under trial at the end of the year	31	17
Percentage of persons convicted to total number tried	63.88	66.9

A decrease of 61 persons is observed in the number of persons brought to trial. 169 cases of petty theft were not enquired into under section 117 of the Criminal Procedure Code. The number is large and section has been taken undue advantage of by the police. Mr. Haris, District superintendent of Police who was specially deputed to report upon the Police of the State, remarked on this point that the percentage of cases not enquired into was larger than in Bengal.

The subjoined statement gives additional details showing the number of persons brought to trial in all courts in cognizable and non-cognizable cases during the past year:[21]

Details	*1879 - 80*	*1880 - 81*

	Cognizable	*Non-Cognizable*	*Cognizable*	*Non-Cognizable*
Cases reported	1,255	1,144	1,034	1,098
Number of persons under trial	871	1,008	814	1,004
Convicted	514	659	548	648
Released	324	339	239	351
Otherwise disposed of.	9	3	13	2
Remaining under trial at the end of the year	24	7	14	3
Percentage of persons convicted to total number tried	61.3	66.03	69.6	64.8

At one time somewhat alarming disturbances took place in consequence of the Census operations but were most energetically and courageously dealt with by the Dewan, the Fouzdari Ahilkar and the Police. Arrests of ringleaders were made, and quiet gradually restored. The Deputy Commissioner himself went out to Chilker Hat in the sudder sub – division and also of some of the northern talooks, where his presence had the effect of restoring order.

There were only 18 criminal appeals during the year against 24 of the previous year. Of the 18, one was pending from the last year. In 10 cases the orders of the lower courts were confirmed and in 5 the orders were reversed. Three appeals were pending at the close of the year. The sub –joined table will show the number of persons convicted and appeals preferred with the result in the case of each officer, separately. The Deputy Commissioner heard 12 and the Fouzdari Ahilkar three appeals during the year.[22]

The statement given below will show the result of

NAME OF OFFICERS	Total number of persons punished	Total No. of appeals	Order confinement	Order modified	Order reversed
Babu Jadab Chandra chakroborty, Fouzdari Ahilkar	232	3	3	----------	--------
Satya Charan mukherjee, Offg., Foudari Ahilkar	82	3	2	-----------	1
Peary Lal Roy, Naib Ahilkar	133	4	2	---------	-------
Hari das Mukherjee, M.A.B.L	59	1	1	----------	--------
Kumar Keshav Narayan, Assistant Fouzdari Ahilkar	274	2	-------	----------	2
Sashi Bhusan Halder, Naib Ahilkar of Dinhata	184	2	1	---------	--------
Kadar Nath Mukherjee, Naib Ahilkar of	145	------	-----	----------	---------
Mathabhanga	59	3	1	----------	2
Kumar Rungila Narayan, ahilkar of Mekhliguni					
TOTAL	1,168	18	10	-------	5

NAME OF OFFICERS	No. of cases	No. of persons under trial	Convicted	Acquited or discharged	Otherwise disposed of.	Remaining under trial at the end of the year	Percentage of cinviction to total number trial	REM
Deputy Commissioner	8	41	28	10	-----	3	73.5	
Jagdish Chandra Chakraborty, Fouzdari	396	332	232	91	2	7	71.8	
Ahilkar	258	132	82	49	1	------	62.5	
Satya Charan Mukherjee, offg. Fouzdari	160	231	133	93	2	3	58.8	
Ahilkar	64	99	59	40	-----	-------	59.5	
Peary lal Roy, Suder Naib ahilkar	282	421	274	145	2	------	65.3	
Hari Das Mukherjee, Aditional Naib Ahilkar	285	96	59	36	1	-------	62.1	
Kumar Keshav Narayan	359	185	145	37	3	-------	79.4	
Kumar Rungula Narayan, Naib Ahilkar	334	281	184	89	4	4	67.3	
Mekhligunj								
Soshi Bhusan Halder, Naib Ahilkar, Dinhata								
TOTAL	2,146	1,818	1,196	590	15	17	66.9	

the commitments to the Sessions :[23]

Names of the commiting officers	No. of persons committed	No. of persons convicted	No. released	Died or escaped	Pending trial	Percentage of conviction
Jadab Chandra Chakraborty, Fouzdari Ahilkar	4	2	1	--------	1	
Satya Chanran Mukherjee, offg. Do do	15	12	3	------	-----	
Kedar Nath Mukherjee, Naib Ahilkar, Mathabhanga	4	1	1	--------	2	
Kumar Rungila Narayan, Naib Ahilkar, Mekhligunj	10	9	1	-----	------	
Soshi Bhusan Halder, Naib Ahilkar, Dinhata	5	4	1	--------	-------	
	38	28	7	----	3	

Security for good behaviour was ordered to be taken from one man during the year. The number in the last year was also one. The Police should have been more active in this important part of the notorious bad characters of thre Raj.

The sub-joined statement will show the result of fine operations during the year under report as compared with previous year:[24]

YEAR	Balance of the previous year			Imposed during the year			Realised during the year			Remitted or written off			Balance at the end of the year		
	Rs.	A.	P.	Rs.	A.	P.	Rs.	A.	P.	Rs.	A.	P.	Rs.	A.	P.
1879-80	2,987	10	5	6,929	6	0	6,143	13	0	1,512	6	6	2,260	12	11
1880-81	2,260	12	11	9,028	6	0	7,071	5	9	1,051	11	6	3,166	1	8

The year ends with a heavier balance (Rs.3,166 – 1 – 8) than that at the end of the year 9Rs. 2,260 – 12 - 11), yet it will be observed that the total amount realized during the year was Rs. 7,071 – 5 – 9 or Rs. 927 – 8 – 9 more than that collected in the previous year. The Fouzdari Ahilkar has satisfied himself that the heavy balance is partly owing to the existence in the fine book of 3 items of fine aggregating Rs. 1,179 – 15, for the realization of which all endeavours have been made to no effect. Two of the defaulters are residents of Government Districts in Bengal and one of Cooch Behar. There is another reason which also tended to swel the amount of the balance, large number of cases were disposed of in the previous year and the amount of fine imposed in these cases alone was Rs. 2,672 -8. There was, therefore, no time left within the year to take step for the realization of the whole of the money.[25]

During the year 1882 – 83 the total number of cognizable and non- cognizable cases reported during the year under report was 2,244 against 2,105 of the previous year, showing an increase of 139 cases; of these 974 were congnizable and 1270 were non –cognizable against 905 and 1200 respectively of the previous year. Cognizable cases have therefore increased by 69 and non–cognizable cases by 70.[26]

YEAR	*OFFENCE*		*TOTAL*
	Cognizable	*Non-Cognizable*	
1880 – 81	1,034	1,098	2,132
1881 – 82	905	1,200	2,105
1882 – 83	974	1,270	2,244

From the statement given above it will be seen that there has been an increase of 139 cases of all descriptions in the year under report. In Mathabhanga alone there has been an increase of 123 cases at Dinhata the increase was 70, while cases have decreased in the sudder station and Mekhligunj by 45 and 9 respectively. The Officer in-charge of the Mathabhanga Sub-division gives the following explanation for the increase. "The year under report was better in respect of harvest and the prices of the good grains and as natural there was an increase in the petty cases of trespass, assault and mischief. There has been a marked increase in the case under Section 456 and 457, which may be thus accounted for. There were instances of cognizable offences in which no information was given to the Police by the aggrieved party and the chowkidars were either quite indifferent or amicably settled the cases in the mofussil.[27] There were some prosecutions under under Section 176 and 202 I.P.C. The Commissioner of the state was impressed upon the Police officers here, the duty of carefully explaining to the chowkidars that they are legally bound to furnish information of cases under Section 457 &c. The result has been that the parties or the chowkidars have been more prompt in giving information, which necessarily brings to light many of the cases, which were formerly never brought under notice."On the other hand the Naib Ahilkar of Dinhata accounts for the increase in the following manner ; " The increase in the total number of offences may appear unsatisfactory at first sight. The number of persons brought to trial, however, and specially of those convicted is less than that in the previous year. The increase is greatest in cognizable cases and that in class 3; but technical burglary is a very common offence here. They used in previous years to be shown under Section 381 I.P.C. The increase should not therefore be regarded as indicative of an extraordinary amount of weakness in ayear which is otherwise conspicuous by the absence of grave offences. There is no doubt, however, that burglary is becoming habitual amongst a certain class of the population."[28]

More or less the experience of the past three years has shown that the hopes then expressed were warranted. The low rate of crime has been maintained.The presure which the enhanced rates of the settlements introduced in 1872, combined with the higher prices, especially of rice, which prevailed after the famine up to 1879, had put upon the lower classes, had passed away. Food is cheap—too cheap indeed for the cultivators interest, though a rice eating country, this of course means abundance of food. There was no pauper class in Cooch Behar. The mass of the people are comfortably off. Their wants were few and within their means. They have no incentive to petty crime.[29] The people of Cooch behar known as Cooch Beharis have been almost exclusively a nation of cultivators, who lived on the products of their fields, selling what they did not require to itinerant Paikars and buying their clothes and paying their rent with the proceeds. Increased facilities of communication beginning to attract outsiders to a country where jute, tobacco and rice were cheap and abundant. Local merchants are settling and opening warehouses and their capital is beginning to flow into the country. Increase of crime will surely follow. So far as professional thieves from other districts can come and get away from the state far more easily and quickly than formerly and burglaries and dacoities are almost sure to increase. Report shows crime may be considered to have reached its lowest ebb in Cooch Behar in so far as property is affected by it. With a railway through the state it will probably increase considerably.[30]

It is true that among the cognizable cases, offences against the State, public tranquility, safety and justice, amounted seven in the year under report against ten of the previous year, showing a decrease of three cases. In at Class II, "serious offences against person", the number was 63 against 67 of the previous year, showing a decrease of 4. An increase of 75 cases under the class "serious offences against property", Class III. In 1881–82, the number was 287 while in the year under review, the number has increased to 362.[31] There was a sudden jump in last year's figures from 48 in 1880 -81 to 287 under this class of offences, owing as was explained to the fact that a large number of cases, which technically came under the dennition of burglary, used to be entered as theft in a building under Section. The changes in the system introduced by Mr. Harris, came into force three months after the commencement of the year under report.[32] Along with it the number of minor offences against person (Class IV) was 94 against 70 of the previous year, showing an increase of 24. There is a decrease of 30 cases in the number of minor offences against property (Class V). The number reported during the year was 427 while it was 457 in the preceeding year; this decrease, accounted for by the increase under Class II. In Class I " offences against the State, public tranquility &c."There has been an increase of 20 cases. The number of cases in class II. "Serious offences against person" only 2 against 4 in the previous year. Offwences under Class III, "serious offences against property", have decreased by 14; the number in the year under report was 4 against 18 of the previous year. Class

IV "minor offences agains tthre person" shows also decrease of 7 cases; the number in the two year were 475 and 468 respectively. Class VI, "other offences not specified above" shows a decrease of 29 cases.[33]

The Comparative Statement of all Courts :[34]

PARTICULARS	*1881 - 82*	*1882 - 83*
Number of cognizable and non–cognizable cases reported	2,105	2,244
Number of persons brought to trial	2,048	2,123
Convicted	1,209	1,278
Released	777	767
Otherwise disposed of	953	870
Remaining under trial at the end of the year		
Percentage of persons convicted to total number tried	60.8	62.4

The number of persons brought to trial in the year under report has increased by 75. The percentage of persons convicted to total number tried was 62.4 against 60.8 of the previous year; 70 persons were pending trial at the end of the year under report against 53 of the previous year. Of these 70, 27 were pending before the Session Court, 19 before the Sudder Magisterial persons pending trial in the Sub-divisional Courts of mathabhanga and Mekhligunj.[35]

The following statement provided a details of the number of persons brought to trial in all Courts in all Courts in cognizable and non-cognizable cases during the past year as compared with the preceding year:[36]

DETAILS	*1881 – 82*		*1882 - 83*	
	Cognizable	*Non-Cognizable*	*Cognizable*	*Non - cognizable*
Cases reported	905	1,200	974	1,270
Number of persons under trial	924	1,124	970	1,153
Convicted	550	659	608	670
Released	324	453	304	463
Othewise disposed of	9	—	6	2

Remaining under trial at the end of the year	41	1	52	18
Percentage of persons convicted to total number under trial	62.9	59.2	66.6	50.3

Regarding appeals there were 36 appeals under report against 16 of the preceding year, showing an increase of 20 cases. In 16 cases the orders of the lower court were confirmed, in 3 cases the orders were modified, in 14 appeals the orders were reversed and 3 cases were pending before the Deputy Commissioner at the end of the year. The following table shows the number of persons convicted and appeals preferred with the result:[37]

NAME OF OFFICERS	Total number of persons punished	Total number of appeals preferred	Order confirmed	Order modified	Order reversed	Pending
Jadab Chander Chukraborty, Fouzdari Ahilkar	126	8	5	1	2	—
Satya Chanran Mukherjee, Offg. Fouzdari Ahilkar	28	1	1	—	—	—
Priya nath Dutt, Naib Ahilkar	5	1	—	—	1	—
Kedar Nath mukherjee, Naib Ahilkar	98	4	3	—	1	—
Krishna Dhana Banerjee, offg. Naib Ahilkar	22	1	—	1	—	—
Kumar Rungila Narayan, Naib Ahilkar	80	4	2	—	2	—
Keshab Narayan, Assistant Fouzdari Ahilkar	290	2	2	—	—	—
Hari Das Mukherjee, Naib Ahilkar Mathabhanga	238	2	—	1	1	—
Rabindra Lall Shome, Naib Ahilkar, Mekhligunj	151	1	—	—	1	—
Girish Chandra Sarkar, Naib Ahilkar, Dinhata	163	12	3	—	6	
TOTAL	1,201	36	16	3	14	3

The following statement shows the distribution of work between the several officers, during the year :[38]

There were altogether 19 cases for disposal during

NAME OR OFFICERS	No. of cases	No. of persons under trial	Convicted	Acquited or discharged	Otherwise disposed of	Remaining under trial at the end of the year	Percentage of conviction to total number of trial	Remarks
Deputy Commissioner	15	78	15	35	1	27	30.0	
Jadab Chander Chukraborty, Fouzdari Ahilkar	361	217	123	80	2	12	60.5	
Satya Chanran Mukherjee, Offg, Fouzdari Ahilkar	76	40	8	12	—	—	70.0	
Priya nath Dutt, Naib Ahilkar	10	12	4	8	—	—	33.3	
Kedar Nath mukherjee, Naib Ahilkar	123	154	97	49	2	6	66.4	
Sita Nath Banerjee, offg. Naib Ahilkar	42	110	73	36	1	—	66.9	
Krishna Dhana Banerjee, offg. Naib Ahilkar	44	63	22	41	—	—	34.9	
Kumar Rungila Narayan, Naib Ahilkar	129	171	76	94	—	1	44.7	
Keshab Narayan, Assistant Fouzdari Ahilkar	408	476	290	186	—	—	60.9	
Hari Das Mukherjee, Naib Ahilkar Mathabhanga	412	280	237	42	1	—	84.9	
Rabindra Lall Shome, Naib Ahilkar, Mekhligunj	262	236	150	85	1	—	63.8	
Girish Chandra Sarkar, Naib Ahilkar, Dinhata	375	259	155	91	—	13	63.8	
Kumar Rungila Narayan, Dinhata	7	11	4	7	—	—	36.3	
Rameshssur Pramanik	10	16	4	1	—	11	80.0	
TOTAL	2273	2123	1278	767	8	70	62.4	

Name of commiting Officers	No. of case	No. of persons committed	No. of persons convicted	No. released	Otherwise disposed	Remaining pending	No. of cases disposed of	No. pending
Jadab Chander Chakraborty, Fouzdari Ahilkar	3	17	2	14	-------	1	2	1
Hari Das Mukherjee, Naib Ahilkar	7	33	11	8	1	13	5	2
Kader Nath mukherjee, Naib Ahilkar	2	18	--------	13	-------	5	1	1
Krishna Dhana Banerjee, offg. Naib Ahilkar	1	1	-------	-------	-------	1	-------	1
Satya Chander Mukherjee, Fouzdari Ahilkar	1	2	------	------	-------	2	-------	1
Kumar Rangila Narayan, Naib Ahilkar	1	1	-------	--------	------	1	------	1
Radhica Lall Shome, Naib Ahilkar, Mekhligunj	3	5	2	------	-------	3	1	2
Girish Chunder Sikdar, Naib Ahilkar, Dinhata	1	1	------	-------	-------	1	-------	1
TOTAL	190	78	15	35	1	27	9	10

the year, of these 4 were committed during the previous year. Nine cases only were disposed of which three were tried by Captain Gordon, four by Dewan and two by Mr. Dalton. The very bad percentage of convictions to acquittals results from the fact that in three cases one of which was tried by Captain Gordon and two by the Dewan, the number of accused were 13, 14 and 7 respectively and all were acquitted.[39]

Five persons were ordered to find security for good behaviour during the year. There were twenty applications for maintenance made during the year; of these four were decided in favour of the applicants, ten refused, three compromised and three applications were pending at the end of the year. Attachment proceedings for the appearance of defendants had to be taken in seven cases during the year under report against three of the preceding year.[40] Rs. 121 -12 were awarded as compensation to defendants under Section 250 Code of Criminal Procedure, against Rs. 114 of the preceding year. Proceedings had to be taken in six cases for the suppression of local nuisances during the year. The number of cases instituted under Section 147 of the Procedure Code for right of way, was 22 against 35 of the previous year. Of these 12 were decided in favour of the plaintiffs, 3 cases were dismissed, 1 compromised and 6 cases remained pending at the end of the year.[41]

The number of accidental deaths reported during the year was 145 against 137 of the previous year, which have been as follows :[42]

Suicide	3
By drowning	77
By snake bite	87
By wild beats	7
Other causes	21
Total	145

Year	Balance of the previous year	Imposed during the year	Realized during the year	Remitted or written off	Balance at the end of the year
	Rs. A. P.	Rs. A. P.	Rs. A. P.	Rs. A. P.	Rs. A. P.
1881 – 82	3,166 1 8	7,573 6 0	7,314 8 1	288 5 6	3,136 10 1
1882 – 83	3,136 10 1	8,469 6 0	7,211 5 3	2,448 9 5	1,946 1 5

The amount realized during the year was Rs. 7,211 – 5 – 3 against Rs. 7,314 – 8 – 1 of the previous year, showing a decrease of Rs. 103 – 2 – 10. The outstanding balance at the end of th eyear was Rs. 1,946 – 1 – 5 against Rs. 3,136 – 10 – 1 of the previous year, showing a decrease of Rs. 1,190 – 8 – 8. The Commissioner has been moved to order the writing off Rs. 1,720 – 10 – 2 which continued unnecessarily to swell the balance of unrealized fines for the last few years. All that could be done has been done to collect this amount, but to no effect. The amount has been deducted from the balance.[43]

Regarding the assessment for the year under review was Rs. 2,162 – 14 against Rs. 2,266 – 5 in the previous year. Such an amount together with Rs. 2 -2 -3 the balance of the previous year, gives a total of Rs. 2,165 – 0 – 3. Deducting from this sum Rs. 113 – 0 – 6 on account of persons who have died or left their place of abode, there remained Rs. 2051 – 15 – 9. Of this amount Rs. 2,051 – 8 – 6 were collected during the year, leaving a balance of annas 7 – 3. The assessment for the past year was less by Rs. 103 – 7 than that for the preceding one. This is due to the fact several tax-payers have been removed from their holdings inside the town, to clear the grounds about the site of the new Palace and for purposes of town improvement. These persons have settled outside the limits to which the chowkidari asssment extended.[44] It will be necessary almost immediately to extend these limits so as to include the bastes, which are forming just outside the existing boundaries. When the railway comes to Cooch Behar, there is no doubt that the population of the town will increase considerably.

On the cost of chowkidari establishment was Rs. 2,038

– 6 – 6. The chowkidars, who get only Rs. 5 a month, are no doubt underpaid when compared with the sweepers of the conservancy Department who get Rs. 7.According to the Fouzdari Ahilkar, it is necessary to place these two bodies of Municipal servants in an equality in point of pay. It is difficult to procure sweepers, hence they command higher pay. There are no indigenous sweepers, but plenty of indigenous chowkidars.[45] The question of a municipality for Cooch Behar is under consideration and the pay and position of the chowkidars would naturally be considered in connection with any scheme that may be put forward for approval.

As per the records shows the number of village chowkidars was 1,576 during the year against 1,664 of the previous year, showing a decrease of 88 men. Such a claculation simply means that some of those who were voluntary supporters of the chowkidari system are getting tired of paying for their protection and that chowkidars have ceased to serve, because they cannot get paid. Commissioner sending up an urgent recommendation for the immediate legislation of compulsory measures to realise chowkidari fees wherever due, and this will be followed by a proposal to introduce a short act both for the control and payment of the force. The movement, out of which the present force has sprung, was a spontaneous one, but the people have taken upon themselves obligations which must be compelled by law to fulfill.[46] Captain Gordon in his report for 1880 – 81 stated that it had been, in which he concurred that any legislation in this direction must be very gradually and carefully under-taken if ultimate success was to be assured. Captain Gordon apparently put a wrong construction in recommending the introduction of an act. Any fresh legislation for the purpose of imposing a tax so soon after the census operations, would be inseparably connected with that event in the minds of the people and as the chowkidari movement was still in full swing and the number of chowkidars increasing under the voluntary system in vogue, it would be a pity to do any thing which might even appear to discredit assertion that no new tax was intended which reiterated on every possible occasion when the enumaretors were doing their work. But the sponteneous action of the people has reached its furthest limits and a reaction is setting in. It is no hardship to blind them to go on doing what thye have commenced of their own accord.[47] It is no longer a new tax, and will not be left as one. Those whomhave never paid will grumble but the great majority of those who would be assessed under a Panchayet system have been paying already for some time with more or less regularity and they will be grateful for a measure which will lighten their burdens in so far as it compels those who have held back to join in taking their fair share of the cost of guarding the community of which they are members against the depredations of the criminal classes. During the year Fouzdari Ahilkar received no fewer than 258 petitions from chowkidar's each containing lists of defaulters who had not paid up their quota of subscription and the complains that the work of his office is seriously increased thereby. Every thing therefore points to the immediate necessity for taking steps to bring the chowkidari system under legal control. Regarding the sub – divisional officers and officers with power of criminal jurisdiction at the Sudder Station :[48]

" Of all the Naib Ahilkars, who exercised criminal powers, Hari Das Mukherjee, Naib Ahilkar of Mathabhanga, deserves special mention.The result of his work, as will appear from the statements in the body of the report, is highlysatisfactory. He tried the largest number of criminal cases but there was not a single case pending before him. The file of the Naib Ahilkar of Dinhata was not at all clear in as much pending before Radhica Lall Shome, the Naib Ahilkar of Mekhligunj. Kumar Keshab Narayan continues to give satisfaction in the quick disposal of petty cases. With the exception of Babu Hari Das Mookherjee, all other officers appear to me to be rather unduly lenient in the punishments awarded by them. I often called their attention to this important matter in my resolutions on the monthly statements, but I fear they have not produced the desired effect. Such punishments as are often awarded by them do in my humble opinion, indirectly encourage people to commit offences."

During the year 1883 – 84, the total number of cognizable and non –cognizable cases reported under report was 2,168 against 2,244 of the previous year, showing a decrease of 76 cases. Of these 1,011 were cognizable and 1,157 were non –cognizable, against 974 and 1,270 respectively of the previous year. Cognizable cases have therefore increased by 37 and non –cognizable cases decreased by 113.[49]

YEAR	*OFFENCES*		*TOTAL*
	Cognizable	*Non-Cognizable*	
1881 – 82	905	1,200	2,105
1882 – 83	974	1,270	2,244
1883 - 84	1,011	1,157	2,168

Among the cognizable cases, "offences against the State, public tranquillity, safety and justice," amounted to 8 in the year under report against 7 of the previous year, showing an increase of 1 case only. In class II, that is " serious offences against person", the number was 82 against 63 of the previous year, showing an increase of 19 cases. An increase of 90 cases is seen under class "serious offences against property", class II. In 1882 -83, the number was 362, while in the year under review, the number has increased to 452. The increase of 90 cases were distributed as under the following heads :[50]

Sudder Tufangunj	40
Dinhata	14
Mathabhanga	45
Total	99
Deduct cases decreased in Mekhligunj	9
Total	90

The increase in "offences against property" is most

probably more apparent than actual, being caused in agreat measure by the operation of the Chowkidari system by which numbers of cases formerly hushed up or remaining unnoticed were reported to the Police. Extracts from reports of the the sub-divisional officers of Mathabhanga and Dinhata as follows :[51]

"Babu Hari Das Mukherjee, the sub-divisional officer of mathabhanga, writes, in my last Annual Report I observed that the increase in the number of cognizable information of the Police, while it appears that in previous years, many of such cases were never brought to light. However, I still suspect that all the cases are not reported to the Police. That remark holds good for the present year too. At the same time it will be remembered that both the Bitri and Haimanti cultivations of the year were not very successful, which served as an additional reason for the increase of the cognizable cases."

The number of "minor offences against the person" class IV, was 15 against 94 of the previous year, showing a decrease of 79 cases. The prevalences of cholera in the State during 4 months from April to July, had doubtless much to do with this decrease. The people were panic stricken and had neither time nor inclination for the commission of offences of this class.[52]

The floowing statement shows the number of cases in each class of Non-cognizable offences. In Class I "Offences against the State, public tranquility" &C, &C. there has been a decrease of 20 cases. There was no case in Class II "serious offences against the property" have increased by 7. The number in the year under report is 11 against 4 of the previous year. Class IV "Minor offences against the person" shows also an increase of 44 cases. The numbers in the two years were 468 and 512 respectively. Minor offences against property Class V, show a decrease of 51 cases. The numbers having been 264 and 213 in the two years respectively. Class IV other offences not specified above, shows a decrease of 71 cases the number in the last year having been 256 against 327 of the previous year. There has been a decrease of 20 cases of "Offences under special Laws", the number in the last year was 39 against 59 of the previous year.[53]

Comparative statement of all Courts :[54]

PARTICULARS	*1882-83*	*1883–84*
Number of Cognizable and Non-cognizable cases reported	2,244	2,168
Number of persons brought to trial	2,123	1,872
Convicted	1,278	1,207
Released	767	687
Otherwise disposed of	8	5
Remaining under trial at the end of the year	70	28
Percentage of persons convicted to total number tried	62.4	65.4

The number of persons brought to trial in the year under report has decreased by 71. The percentage of conviction to total number tried was 65.4 against 62.4 of the previous year. It shows certainly an improvement and that a greater care and attention has been bestowed upon the examination of complaints and the discovery and admission of true cases. 22 persons in 6 cases were pending trial at the end of the year under report against 70 of the previous year. Of these 22, 5 were pending before the session Court, 5 before the Fouzdari Ahilkar, 4 before the Dinhata Sub-divisional Court and * before the Naib Ahilkar of Mathabhanga. The files were therefore remarkably clear in as much as out of a total of 2168 cases of all descriptions only 6 cases remained undisposed of at the end of the year.

The number of cases not enquired into by the Police under section 157 of the Criminal Procedure Code was 47 against 26 of the previous year.

Details of the all Courts:[55]

DETAILS	*1882 – 83*		*1883 - 84*	
	Cognizable	*Non-Cognizable*	*Cognizable*	*Non-Cognizable*
Cases reported	974	1,270	1,011	1,157
Number of persons under trial	970	1,153	970	1,082
Convicted	608	670	513	694

Released	304	463	26	375
Otherwise disposed of	6	2	2	3
Remaining under trial at the end of the year	5	18	130	10
Percentage of persons convicted to toal number under trial	66.6	50.3	66.1	64.9

There were 45 appeals during the year against 36 of the preceding year, an increase has been noticed of 9 cases. These together with three appeals pending from the year before last, made a total of 48 appeals in all. In 20 cases the orders of the lower Courts were confirmed, in 9 cases the orders were modified, in 15 appeals the orders were reversed and 4 cases were pending at the end of the year, viz., 1 case before the Fouzdari Ahilkar and 3 before the Superintendent of the State. The following table shows the number of persons convicted and appeals preferred with the result in the case of each officer separately.[56] The Superintendent heard 19 appeals And Fouzdari Ahilkar 25.

The distribution of work in between several officers

Name of Officers	Total number of persons punished	Total number of appeals preferred	Order confirmed	Order modified	Order reversed	Pending
Jadab Chander Chakraborty, Fouzdari Ahilkar	207	11	3	2	3	3
Kedar Nath mukherjee, Naib Ahilkar	26	3	2		1	
Kumar Rungila Narayan, Naib Ahilkar	216	6	4	1	2	
Keshav Narayan , Assistant Ahilkar	254	5	3	5	1	1
Kedar nath mukherjee, Naib Ahilkar, Dinhata	129	7	4		3	
Girish Chandra Sarkar, Naib Ahilkar ditto	14	9	2		2	----
Hari Das Mukherjee, Mathabhanga	188	4	2	1 --------	1	
Rameswar Pramanik	26	1	----------	--------	1	---------
Radhica Lall Shome, Naib Ahilkar, Mekhligunj	63	2	-----------		1	--------
TOTAL	1,123	48	20	9	15	4

were as follows :[57]

NAME OF OFFICERS	No. of cases	No. of persons under trial	Convicted	Acquitted or discharged	Otherwise disposed of	Remaining under trial at the end of the year	Percentage of conviction to total number trial	Remarks
Deputy commisioner and Superintendent	11	49	2	17	2	5	59.5	
Jadab Chander Chakraborty, Fouzdari Ahilkar	449	320	207	108	——	5	62.8	
Kumar Rungila Narayan, Naib Ahilkar								
Kumar Keshav Narayan, Assistant Ahilkar	294	385	216	167	2	——	56.3	
Priya Nath Dutt, Naib Ahilkar	386	391	254	136	1	——	65.1	
Kedar Nath mukherjee, Naib Ahilkar	2	6	1	5	——	——	16.6	
Sub-Division Dinhata	31	54	26	28	——	——	48.03	
Kedar nath mukherjee, Naib Ahilkar								
Girish Chandre Sirkar, Naib Ahilkar	306	185	129	52	——	4	71.2	
Rameswar Pramanik, Naib Ahilkar	68	3	14	9	——	——	60.4	
Sub-Division Mathabhanga								
Hari Das Mukherjee, Naib Ahilkar	7	14	11	3	——	——	78.5	
Rameswar Pramanik, Naib Ahilkar	340	47	188	51	——	8	78.7	
Sub-Division Mekhligunj								
Radhika Lal Shome, Naib Ahilkar	48	30	6	4	——	——	86.6	
Rameswar Pramanik, Naib Ahilkar								
	135	110	63	47	——	——	57.2	
	95	58	47	10	——	1	82.4	
TOTAL	2,172	1,872	1,207	637	5	3	65.4	

The following table shows the result of commitment of the Session :[58]

Name ofcommiting Officers	No. of cases	No. of persons cimmited	No. of persons convicted	No. released	Otherwise disposed of	Remaining pending	Percentage of convictions
Jadab Chander Chakraborty, Fouzdari Ahilkar	5	14	6	5	1	2	54.5
Satya chanran Mukherjee, Offg., Fouzdari Ahilkar	1	2	2	-------	-------	-------	100
Kumar Rangila Narayan,Naib Ahilkar	2	2	2	------	-------	-------	100
Krishna Dhana Banerjee, offg., Naib Ahilkar	1	1	1	------	------	-------	100
Kedar Nath Mukherjee, Naib Ahilkar	1	5	4	1	-------	--------	80
Hari Das Mukherjee, Naib Ahilkar, Mathabhanga	7	20	8	9	1	2	47.5
Radhika Lal Shome,Naib Ahilkar, Mekhligunj	2	3	2	1	-------	-------	66.6
Rameswar Pramanik, Naib Ahilkar, Mekhligunj	1	1	-------	-------	--------	1	-------
Girish Chandra sarkar, Naib Ahilkar, Dinhata	1	1	-------	1	-------	-------	------
TOTAL	21	49	25	17	2	5	59.5

Another table shows the result of the operations as reported, compared with the preceding year :[59]

YEAR	Balance of the previous year	Imposed during the year	Realized during the year	Remitted or written off	Balance at the end of the year
	Rs. A. P.	Rs. A. P.	Rs. A. P.	Rs. A. P.	Rs. A. P.
	3,136 10 1	8,469 6 0	7,211 5 3	2,448 9 5	1,946 14 8
	1,946 1 5	7,855 14 0	6,942 0 9	80 0 0	

The amount realized during the year was Rs. 6,942 – 0 – 9 against Rs. 7,211 – 5 – 3 shows a decrease of Rs. 269 – 4 -6. The outstanding balance at the end of the year was Rs. 2,779 -14 – 8 against Rs. 1,946 – 1 -5, an increase of Rs. 833 -13 – 3. The Court Sub-Inspector of the Sudder Court and the Mufassil Naib Ahilkars had submitted lists of fines amounting in all to Rs. 695 – 9 – 2 recommended to be written off. On a close enquiry it appeared that every one of these fines was of less than six years standing and no very cogent reasons were shown for their remission. Lists have therefore been returned for the adoption of more stringent measures for recovery.

During the year 1884 – 85 the charge of the Fouzdari Court rested with Jadab Chunder Chukerbutty, from the beginning of the year to the 6th February 1885. On the 7th February, this officer took privilege leave for 2 months and 3 days and Narendra Nath Sen, M.A., B.L., Sudder Naib Ahilkar, remained in charge up to the 24th idem, when Babu Satya Charan Mukherjee, Superintendent of Police was appointed to officiate as Fouzdari Ahilkar. Regarding the charge of the Sub- divisional Court of Dinhata remained with Babu Kedar Nath Mukherjee, Naib Ahilkar, throughout the year. Babu Hari Das Mukherjee, Naib Ahilkar, was in charge of the Mathabhanga sub- division from the 1st of April to the 24th of June last. He was succeeded by Bubu Rameswar Pramanik on the 25th June, who again was relieved by Babu Sita charge of the Sub-division till the end of the year.[60] The charge of the Mekligunj Sub-division remained with Babu Rameshwar Pramanik from the beginning of the year to the 23rd of June. From the 24th

June to the end of the year, Kumar Rungila Narayan held charge of the Sub-division.

Regarding the total number of cognizable and non-cognizable cases, reported during the year under report was 2410 against 2168 of the previous year, showing an increase of 242 cases; of these 1,211 were cognizable and 1,199 were non-cognizable, against 1,011 and 1,157 respectively of the previous year. Cognizable cases have therefore increased by 200 and non–cognizable cases by 42.[61]

YEAR	OFFENCE		TOTAL
	Cognizable	*Non-Cognizable*	
1882 – 83	974	1,270	2,244
1883 – 84	1,011	1,157	2,168
1884 – 85	1,211	1,199	2,410

From the statement, given above, it will be seen that there has been an increase of 242 cases of all descriptions in the year under report.

Amongst the cognizable cases "offences against the State, public tranquility, safety and justice" amounted to 14 in the year under report against 8 in the previous year, an increase of 6 cases. It may be observed here that 5 out of the 6 were offences agaionst coin. The offenders had rubbed copper pieces with quick- silver and attempted to pass them for silver coins.[62]

In Class II, that was "serious offences against person" the number was 116 against 82 of the previous year showing an increase of 34 cases. Of the 34 cases 11 were complaints of rape under Section 376, and 21 were offences under Section 354 viz. : ——assulting a woman with intent to outrage her modesty and 353, viz, : ——— using criminal force to a public servant, &c. It is worthy of remark that 15 of these cases were proved to be false.

An increase of 3 cases only is seen under Class III "serious offences against property." The number of "minor offences against the person" Class IV was 24 against 15 of the previous year showing an increase of 9 cases. There is an increase of 141 cases in the number of minor offences against property (Class V).[63] The number reported during the year under report was 582, while it was 441 in the preceeding year. This increase of 141 cases were chiefly attributable to the partial failure of crops and the consequent rise in the price if articles of food.

In the sub –division of Dinhata alone, there has been an increase of 5 cases. The Naib Ahilkar thinks that the above causes have much to do with it. There was a greater failure of crops in Dinhata than in any other division of the State. The number of cases in each class of non – cognizable offence. In Class I "offences against the State, public tranquility &c., &c, there has been an increase of 32 cases; most of these cases were of a triffling nature, such as non-attendance by witnesses in obedience to summons &c. There was no case in Class II 'serious offences against the person", Offences under Class III "serious offences against property" have decreased by 2. The number in the year under report was 9 against 11 of the previous year. Class IV "minor offences against the person" shows an increase of 32 cases. The numbers in the 2 years under comparision were 512 and 544 respectively. "minor offences against property", Class V, show an increase of 17 cases. The number having been 213 and 230 in the 2 years respectively.[64]

Comparative statement of all Courts:[65]

PARTICULARS	*1883 – 84*	*1884 – 85*
Number of Cognizable and Non-Cognizable cases reported	2,168	2,410
Number of persons brought to trial	1,872	2,175
Convicted	1,207	1,246
Released	637	786
Otherwise disposed of	5	10
Remaining under trial at the end of the year	23	133
Percentage of persons convicted to total number tried	65.4	61.3

The number of persons brought to trial in the year under report has increased by 303. The percentage of conviction to total number tried, was 61.3 against 65.4 of the previous year. This falling off in the percentage of conviction was partly attributable to the frequent change of Magisterial officers. According to the report and partly to the indiscriminate summoning of accused persons with out a sufficiently careful examination of the complainants by some of the officers.[66] The attention of all the subordinate Magisterial officers will be called to this point. Circulars with detailed directions as to how these examinations must be conducted were issued from time to time for the guidance of the criminal Courts. 133 persons in 48 cases were pending trial at the end of the year under review against 22 of the previous year, of these 11 were pending before the session Court, 34 before the officiating Fouzdari Ahilkar Babu Satya Chanran Mukherjee, 2 before Babu Hari Das Mukherjee, Sudder Naib Ahilkar, 28 before Parbutty chanran Chukerbutty, officiating naib Ahilkar of Dinhata, 11 before the Naib Ahilkar of Mathabhanga and 2 before the Naib Ahilkar of Mekhligunj.[67]

The fact that such a large number of person were awaiting trial at the end of the year was similarly owing to the frequent change of officers during the year. Certain cases involving large numbers of persons were sent up by the Police at the end of the year and they could not therefore be disposed of during the year under report. The Naib Ahilkar of Dinhata states in explanation. "It is to be observed that most of the cases were challanged by the Police at the close of the year when there was not sufficient time to examine witnesses for prosecution as well as defence."[68] The number of cases not enquired into by the Police under Section 157 of the Criminal Procedure Code was 52 against 47 of the previous year.

Details Statement of all Court:[69]

DETAILS	*1883 – 84*		*1884 – 85*	
	Cognizable	*Non-Cognizable*	*Cognizable*	*Non-Cognizable*
Cases reported	1,011	1,157	1,211	1,199
Number of persons under trial	790	1,082	1,057	1,118
Convicted	513	694	580	666
Released	262	375	366	420

Otherwise disposed of	2	3	10	—
Remaining under trial at the end of the year	130	10	101	3
Percentage of persons convicted to total number under trial	66.1	64.9	61.3	61.3

There were 5 cases of murder, involving 6 persons, reported during the year under review against 3 of the previous year. There were two cases of culpable homicide not amounting to murder reported during the year under review, against none in the preceding year of which one was found false by the Naib Ahilkar of Mathabhanga and in the other, 8 persons have been committed to the sessions by the Fouzdari Ahilkar, they were awaiting trial before that Court. The history of the true case is as follows :[70]

One Dina Nath Das of Kaljani, Kotwali Station, left his home for the purpose of realizing dues from a fellow–villager, Kola Nath Deori and as he had not returned by the afternoon of the next day, suspicion arose in the mind of his brother Gooneshwar Das, who set out to search for him and found his body under a Hejul tree. He at once lodged information with the Police. The decreased had an intrigue with Rothy Dassia, the wife of his fellow-villager Neel Chand Das and when he Dina Nath, was in his paramour's house at night Neel Chand was awoke by a clattering noise and Seized Dina Nath, calling out to his next door neighbour.[71] Shib Nath Deori, saying that a man had entered the house; Shib Nath came up and was followed by Garo Daffadar. Poran Das, Chandra Nath Das, Ram pershad Pundit, Fool Chand das and Shurba Chowkidar; they all then beat Dina Nath and brought him into the yard where he dit and Fook Chand then carried the body away in a bag. The Police sent up the eight persons for trial, of whom accused Neel Chand Das and Poran Das have confessed and implicated Shib Das and five others; they were all committed to the Sessions and were awaiting trial at the close of the year. There were 51 appeals during the year under report against 45 of the preceding year, showing an increase of 6 appeals. These together with the 4 appeals pending from the year before last, made a total of 55 appeals in all. In 28 cases the orders of the Lower Court were confirmed, in 5 cases the orders were modified, in 14 appeals, the orders were reversed, in 3 cases the appeals were rejected and 5 cases were pending at the end of the year. Viz, 3 cases before the Fouzdari Ahilkar and 2 before the Superintendent of the state.[72] From the following table shows the number of persons convicted and appeals preferred with the result in the cases of each officer separately.[73] The Superintendent of the state heard 10 appeals and the Fouzdari Ahilkar 40.

NAME OF OFFICERS	Total number of persons punished	Total number of appeals	Order confirmed	Appeal rejected	Order modified	Order reversed	Pending
Jadab Chander Chaukroborty, Fouzdari Ahilkar	185	11	5	2	1	2	1
Hari Das Mukherjee, Sudder Naib Ahilkar	6	1	-------	-----	-----	-------	1
Kumar Rungila Narayan, Sudder Naib Ahilkar	23	7	5	-----	-----	2	------
Narendra Nath Sen, Sudder Naib Ahilkar	103	5	5	-----	-----	-----	------
Purbatty Charan Chukraborty, offg. Naib Ahilkar	20	1	-------	----	-----	-----	1
Kumar Keshab Narayan, Assistant Ahilkar	354	15	5	1	3	5	1
Mekhligunj							
Rameshwar Pramanik, Naib Ahilkar	16	2	-------	-----	------	2	-----
Kumar Rungila Narayan, Ditto							
Mathabhanga	78	1	------	-----	1	------	-----
Hari Das Mukherjee, Naib Ahilkar							
Rameshwar Pramanik	25	1	------	-----	-----	1	------
Dinhata	54	3	3	------	------	------	-----
Kedar Nath Mukherjee	189	8	5	-----	-----	2	1
TOTAL	1,053	55	28	3	5	14	5

The Statement given below shows the distribution of work in between several officers:[74]

NAMES OF OFFICERS	No. of cases	No. of person under trial	Convicted	Acquitted or discharged	Otherwise disposed of	Remaining under trial at the end of the year	Percentage of conviction to total number trial	Remarks
Superintendent of the State	11	38	22	4	1	11	84.6	
Jadab Chander Chukroborty, Fouzdari Ahilkar	428	304	185	117	2	-----	61.2	
Satya Chanran Mukherjee, offg. Fouzdari Ahilkar	74	63	20	8	1	34	71.4	
Hari das Mukherjee, Sudder Naib Ahilkar	17	28	6	20	------	2	23.07	
Kumar Rungila Narayan, ditto	52	51	23	28	------	------	45.09	
Narendra Nath Sen, ditto	164	181	103	73	5	------	58.5	
Parbotty Charan Chakraborty, Offg. Naib Ahilkar	39	60	20	10	------	30	66.6	
Kumar keshab Narayan, Assistant Ahilkar	556	649	354	267	------	28	57.04	
Sub –division Dinhata								
Kedar nath mukherjee, Naib Ahilkar	433	269	189	65	------	15	74.4	
Sub –Division Mathabhanga								
Hari Das Mukherjee, Naib Ahilkar	64	37	25	12	------	------	67.5	
Rameswar pramanik, Naib Ahilkar	113	61	54	7	------	------	88.5	
Sita Nath Banerjee, Naib Ahilkar	237	255	151	92	1	11	62.1	
Sub-Division Mekhligunj								
Rameshwar Pramanik, Naib Ahilkar	35	5	16	9	------	----	64	
Kumar Rungila Narayan, Naib Ahilkar	209	154	78	74	-------	2	51.3	
TOTAL	2,432	2,175	1,246	786	10	133	61.3	

The following table shows the result of commitment to the Sessions :[75]

Name of the Committing Officers	No. of cases	No. of persons committed	No. of persons convicted	No. of persons released	Otherwise disposed of	Remaining pendings	Percentage of convictions
Jadab Chander Chakraborty, Fouzdari Ahilkar	6	6	4	2	-------	---------	66.6
Satya Charan Mukherjee, Fouzdari Ahilkar	1	9	------	-------	--------	9	-------
Hari Das Mukherjee, Naib Ahilkar, Mathabhanga	3	3	2	1	-------	------	66.6
Sita Nath Mukherjee, Ditto	2	2	1	--------	1	------	100
Kedar Nath Mukherjee, Naib Ahilkar,Dinhata	3	17	14	1	-------	2	23.3
Rameswar pramanik, Mekhligunj	1	1	1		--------	------	100
TOTAL	16	38	22	4	1	11	84.6

Rs. 75 were awarded as compensation to defendants under section 250 of the Criminal Procedure Code against Rs. 73 of the preceding year. There was no case in which proceedings had to be taken for the suppression of local nuisance under Section 143 of the criminal Procedure Code. The number of cases instituted under Section 147 of the Code of Criminal Procedure for right of way was 27 against 20 of the proceeding year, of these eight were decided in favour of the plaintiff, six cases were dismissed seven compromised and six pending.

The number of accidental deaths reported during the year was 131 against 160 of the previous year showing a decrease of 29. They were stated to have been as follows:[76]

Suicide	6
By drowning	74
By snake –bite	23
By wild beasts	6
By other causes	22
Total	131

The table given below shows the result of fine operations during the year under report as compared with the preceeding year :[77]

YEAR	Balance of the previous year		Imposed during the year		Realised during the year		Remitted or written off		Balance at the end of the year	
	Rs.	A. P.	Rs.	A. P.	Rs.	A. P.	Rs.	A. P.	Rs.	A. P.
1883 -84	1,946	1 5	7,855	14 0	6,942	0 9	80	0 0	2,779	14 8
1884 -85	2,779	14 8	6,894	0 0	6,223	11 0	1,216	2 0	2,234	1 8

The amount released during the year was Rs. 6,223 – 11 against Rs. 6,942 – 0 – 9 showing a decrease of Rs. 718 – 5 – 9. Partial failure of crops and the consequent rise in the price of the articles of food have largely affected the fine operations of the year under record.

The following table shows the value of stamps and Court –fees in the different Criminal Courts during the year under review :[78]

Names of Courts	Stamps			Court -fees			TOTAL		
Sudder Fouzdari Ahilkar	2,100	0	0	1,022	0	0	3,122	0	0
Dinhata Court	487	0	0	431	4	0	918	4	0
Mathabhanga Court	601	0	0	350	12	0	351	12	0
Mekhligunj Court	234	0	0	156	12	0	390	12	0
TOTAL	3,422	0	0	1,960	12	0	5,382	12	0

The number of persons examined (complainants, witnesses and accused) was 8379.

Regarding miscellaneous work in 1884 -85, the different Criminal Courts were as follows :[79]

Names of Courts	No. of petitions received	No. of order passed	No. of process of all kinds of issues	No. of reports heard	No. of robocaries issued	No. of robocaries received	No. of bail-bond executed	No. of recognizance
Sudder Fouzdari Ahilkar Sudder Naib Ahilkar Sudder Assistant Ahilkar	2138	857	4,338	11,893	397	234	338	721
Dinhata Court	647	367	985	345	48	223	57	201
Mathabhanga Court	761	930	2,878	876	79	86	55	455
Mekhligunj Court	437	255	484	220	30	150	90	103
TOTAL	3,983	2,409	8,685	13,334	554	693	540	1,480

Thre number of English letters despatched and received in the Sudder Fouzdari Court was 589 and 380 respectively. The assessment for the year under report was Rs. 1,962 – 12 against Rs. 2,050 in the previous year. Such an amount together with Rs. 293 – 9 the tax assessed on the new houses and annas 1 – 3 the balance of the previous year, gives a total of Rs. 2,256 – 6 – 3. Deducting from this sun Rs.99 – 11 – 6 on account of persons who have either died or left their places of abode there remained Rs.2,156 -10 – 9. Of this amount, Rs. 1,803 – 15 were collected during the year leaving a balance of Rs. 352 – 11 – 9. It was proposed that the Town Committee Act should come into operation during the latter half of the year under report. As a fresh assessment of the taxes would have been necessary in that case it was thought advisable to realize the tax for three quarters of the year only during the last year. Hence the heavy balance that remained unrealized at the end of the year.

The Fouzdari Ahilkar reports as follows :[80]

> "One sub–inspector, two Head–constables and 12 constables were judicially punished during the year under report against six head –constables and 19 constables of the previous year. Sub –inspector Guru Prasanna Singha and Head–constable Mokhtearuddin have done excellent service during the year under report. The former has already been rewarded by His Highness in Council by the grant of a permanent increment of Rs. 10 to his pay; but the latter's services remain yet unrewarded. He is an old Police officer of 17 years standing and successffuly enquired into no less than 15 theft cases during the year. Several gangs of thieves in the neighbourhood of the sudder station were brought to justice by the Head –constable. The first vacancy in the post of a Sub – Inspector should be filled up by giving him a promotion which he so richly deserves. In

> my letter No. 441, dated the 4th December 1884, I had called the attention of the Superintendent of Police to the services of the Head–constable."

There were 80 petitions from husbands to regain possession of their wives during the year. In 48 cases the wives were made over to their husbands; 25 petitions were struck off in default, most probably the wives returned to their husbands of their own accord. In 7 cases, the wives (all nica–wives) denied the fact of their marriage with the petitioners and the husbands were referred to the Civil Courts to establish their marriage.

The Fouzdari Ahilkar was invested with summary powers in August 1884. The number of cases tried him summarily during the year was 13 only.

The Fouzdari Ahilkar reports as follows :[81]

"The number of chowkidars (1,578) remained the same during the year under report. Towards the end of the year, 2 chowkidars in the jurisdiction of the Haldibari Station were dismissed. Their placess were not filled up duriong the year. The number of petitions received during thre year for the realization of the chowkidar's pay was 560 against 314 of the preceeding year, showing an increase of 246 petitions. Formerly these petitions used to be sent to the Police Stations, who deputed constables for the realization of the money. The constables used to make the payment to the chowkidars at once. Petitions were received by me from which it appeared, that in some cases, the total amounts realized did not find their way to the chowkidars. I therefore made a rule that the Police must pay down every pic, they realized to the Court Sub – Inspector's office. A cash book has been opened in which these amounts are credited. The money is then given to the Chowkidar on a regular receipt. As a rule, the chowkidars come with the money and are then and there paid away; whenever there is a delay, an order is sent to the Police to bring up the Chowkidar who is produced in Court and paid off. Rs. 2,216 -14 – 3 were realized during the last year in the Sudder station and were paid down to the chowkidars on receipt. The following amounts were realised in the 3 Subdivisions :[82]

Name of the sub–divisions	*Realised*			*Paid off*		
Mathabhanga ————	1,119	9	6	1,119	9	6
Mekhligunj - ————	553	7	3	553	7	3
Dinhata ————	1,341	14	9	1,341	14	9

In all Rs. 5,231 – 13 – 9 were realised and paid off during the year on account of the pay of the chowkidars. The work of the department has nearly doubled during the year, as already brought to the notice of the authorities the necessity of appointing a Moherer for the Department."

In 1891 - 92 recods shows that Babu Priya Nath Dutt, M.A., B.L., Fouzdari Ahilkar was in charge of the Sudder Fouzdari Office throughout the year. He was assisted by Sub Naib–Ahilkar, Babu Sathish Chander Mustafi, thoughout the year by Sudder Sub-Naib Ahilkar, bau Harendra Narayan Chowdhuri, B.L., from the beginning of the year to the 18th December and by Moulavi Yaquiddin Ahmed, B.L., from the 19th December to the end of the year. The last two officers exercised the powers of a Magistrate of the 2nd class and did criminal work in addition to their duties in the Civil Department.[83]

The charge of the Sub–division of Dinhata remained with Babu Surapati Chatterjee, B.L., from the beginning of the year to the 12th June and with Babu Ramwshwar Pramanik, B.L., from the 13 th June to the close of the year. These officers were assisted by Sub–Naib Ahilkar, Babu Jogendra Nath Sanyal went away on leave and died. The post of Sub–Naib Ahilkar remained vacant from thre 18th September to the 15th of November, Babu Purna Chandra Mitter, B.L., officiating naib Ahilkar, assumed charge of his duties on the 16th November and continued in charge till the end of the year.[84]

On the other hand Babu Sita Nath Banerjee, naib Ahilkar was in charge of the Sub-division throughout the year. He was assisted by Babu Ashutosh Ghosh, B.L., from the beginning of the year to the 23rd of December and by Babu Harendra Narayan Chowdhuri, B.L., from the 24th of December to the 31st of march 1892.[85]

Moulvie Yaquinuddir Ahmed, B.L., was in charge of this Sub–division from the 1st April to the 12th of September to the end of the year.[86]

The following table shows the number of cognizable and nno –cognizable cases reported during the last 3 years:[87]

YEAR	*OFFENCE*		*TOTAL*
	Cognizable	*Non-Cognizable*	
1889 – 90	1,337	1,461	2,798
1890 – 91	1,227	1,209	2,436
1891 – 92	1,231	1,311	2,575

The number of cases reported during the year was 2,575 against 2,436 of the previous year, showing an increase of 139 cases. Of these 1,231 were cognizable and 1,344 non –cognizable against 1,227 and 1,209, respectively of the preceding year. It is satisfactory to note that although the prices of food –grains were very high during the year, crime was normal, the increase in the number of cognizable cases being only 4. As regards non –cognizable cases, the increase is mainly attributable to cases under the special laws.

Of the cognizable offences, " offences against the State, public tranquillity, safety and justice" (Vide Class I, statement A, Part I) amounted to 26 against 30 of the previous year, showing an increase of 4 cases. There were 20 cases of unlawful assembly or rioting against 23 and 1 case under offences relating to coin, stamps and Government notes, against the same number of the previous year.[88]

Under Class II of, "Serious offences against person", the number was 81 against 103 of the previous year, showing a satisfactory decrease of 22 cases homicide, 7 of rape and 12 of kidnapping during the previous year. There was no case of unnatural offence during the year against 3 of the preceding year.[89]

Under Class III, i.e. "Serious Offences against property."

There were 361 cases against 408 of the previous year, showing a decrease of 47 cases. This is a most satisfactory decrease in view of the straitened circumstances of the people ——— the result of the year's failure of crops.[90]

Class IV, "Minor offences against person", the number of cases under this head during the year was 65 against 37 of the previous year. There was 63 cases of wrongful restraint and confinement against 36 of the previous year showing an increase of 27 cases.[91]

Class V, "Minor offence against property", there were 671 cases reported during the year against 622 reported during the year before, showing an increase of 49 cases. The number of theft (ordinary) reported during the year was 383 against 329 reported during 1890 -91. The case of cattle lifting during the year werer 23 against 15 of the previous year and that of criminal trespass 202 against 218.[92]

There were 27 cases under offences were recorded against the same number of the previous year.

Statement A, Part II, shows the number of cases under each class of non –cognizable offences.

In Class I "Offences against the state Public tranquility" &c. There were 75 cases against 71 showing an increase of 4 cases only.

In Class II "Serious offences against property". There was no case during the year against 2 of the previous year.

In Class III, "Serious offences against property". There were 21 cases against 13 of the previous year, showing an increase of 8 cases.

In Class IV, "Minor offences against person." There were 566 cases against 545, and in Class V "Minor offences against property". There were 252 cases against 275 of the previous year.

Class VI "Other offences not specified above". Shows an increase of 43 cases.

The number of cases tried under the special laws

during the year was 141 against 57 of the previous year, shows an increase of 84 cases. This was due, in agreat measure, to the introduction of certain bye –laws by the Cooch Behar Town Committee.

The following table shows the number of cases reported and the number of persons brought to trial in all courts during the past and preceeding year :[93]

PARTICULAR	*1890 - 91*	*1891 - 92*
Number of Cognizable and Non–Cognizable cases	2,436	2,575
Number of persons brought to trial	1,676	1,883
Convicted	827	923
Released	676	827
Otherwise disposed of	6	11
Remaining under trial at the end of the year	167	122
Percentage of persons convicted to total number tried	55.2	25.74

The number of persons brought to trial during the year was 1,883 against 1,676 of the previous year, shows an increase of 207 persons.

One humdred and twenty two persons in 65 cases were pending trial at the end of the year under record against 167 persons in 97 cases of the previous year. Of these 122 persons, 11 were pending trial before the Sessions Judge 46 before the Sudder Sub Naib Ahilkar, Moulvie Yaquinnddin Ahmed; 17 before Babu Satish Chunder Mustafi, Sub Naib Ahilkar; 1 before Babu Monmohan Buxi, member of the Cooch Behar Town Committee; 14 before Babu Rameshwar Pramanik, Naib Ahilkar Dinhata; 19 before Babu Purna Chander Mitter, Sub Naib Ahilkar, Dinhata; 6 before Babu Sitanath Banerjee, Naib Ahilkar, Mathabhanga; 3 before babu Surapati Chattarjee, naib Ahilkar, Mekhligunj; and 9 before Babu Priya Nath Dutt, Fouzdari Ahilkar, Sudder. The number of cases not enquired into under Section 157 of the Code of Criminal Procedure was 22 against the same number of the previous year.[94]

The Statement given below shows the details of the number of persons brought to trial in all courts in cognizable cases during the year as compared with the preceeding year :[95]

DETAILS	1890 – 91		1891 – 92	
	Cognizable	Non-Cognizable	Cognizable	Non-Cognizable
Cases Reported	1,227	1,209	1,231	1,344
Number of persons brought to trial	861	815	909	974
Convicted	399	428	399	524
Released	327	349	415	412
Otherwise disposed of	3	3	6	5
Remaining under trial at the close of the year	132	35	89	33
Percentage of persons convicted to total number tried	54.95	55.08	49.01	55.98

The percentage of convictions in cognizable cases fell from 54.95 to 49.01 while in non-cognizable cases it was almost the same for both years.

There were 92 appeals during the year, including two pending from the previous year, from the previous year against 76 of 1890-91 shows an increase of 16 appeals. Of these 18 were heard by the Court of Sessions and 74 by the Fouzdari Ahilkar. The decisions of the Lower Courts were confirmed in 67 cases, modified in 8 and reveresed in 15, while 2 appeals were rejected. The following table shows the number of persons convicted and appeals preferred, with the result in the case of each officer separately :[96]

The following table provided the result of commitments

NAME OF OFFICERS	Total number of persons punished	Total No. of appeals	Order confirmed	Appeals rejected	Order modified	Order reversed	Pending
Sudder							
Priya Nath Dutt, Fouzdari Ahilkar	83	18	16	—	2	—	—
Harendra Narayan Chowdhuri, Sudder Sub Naib Ahilkar	115	18	12	1	3	2	—
Moulevi Yajuinnuddin Ahamed, Sudder Sub Naib Ahilkar	29	4	3	—	—	1	—
Satish Chander Mustafi, Sub Naib Ahilkar	161	9	5	1	1	2	—
Dinhata							
Sarapati Chatterjee, Naib Ahilkar	9	5	2	—	—	3	—
Rameswar Pramanik, Naib Ahilkar	67	19	14	—	1	4	—
Jogendra Nath Sanyal, Offg. Sub Naib Ahilkar	11	2	—	—	1	1	—
Purna Chander Mitter, Offg. Sub Naib Ahilkar	7	1	1	—	—	—	—
Mathabhanga							
Sita Nath Banerjee, Naib Ahilkar	107	5	5	—	—	—	—
Asutosh Ghosh, Sub Naib Ahilkar	50	6	6	—	—	—	—
			1	—	—	1	—
Mekhligunj	54	2	2	—	—	1	—
Moulvie Yajuinnddin Ahamed, Naib Ahilkar	7	3					
Serajuti Chatterjee, Naib Ahilkar							
TOTAL	765	92	67	2	8	15	-------

The following table shows the distribution of work amounted the several officers :[97]

Names of officers	No. of cases	No. of persons under trial	Convicted	Acquitted or discharged	Otherwise disposed of	Remainder under trial at the end of the trial	Percentage of conviction to trial number tried	Remarks
Colonel A. Evans Gordon, Superintendant of the State & Session Judge	4	7	6	1	----	--------	85.71	
Rai Calica Das Dutt, Bahadur, Dewan of the State & Additional Sesson Judge	8	24	16	8	--------	------	66.66	
Judab Chunder Chakraborty, Session Judge	9	27	8	8	------	11	30.00	
Priya Nath Dutt, Fouzdari Ahilkar	577	170	83	82	------	5	50.30	
Harendra Narayan Chjowdhuri, Offg. Sudder Naib Ahilkar	201	238	115	123	------	------	48.31	
Moulavie Yajuinnidun Ahmed,offg. Sudder Naib Ahilkar	89	126	29	51	------	46	36.25	
Satish Chander Mustafi, Sudder Naib Ahilkar	402	383	161	201	4	17	44.47	
Monuiddin Baxi , Cooch behar Town Committee	104	107	104	2	------	1	98.11	
Sub – Division Dinhata								
Surapati Chatterjee, Naib Ahilkar	79	23	9	14	------	------	39.13	

Rameswar Pramanik, Naib Ahilkar	326	125	67	44	——	11	60.36	
Jogendra Nath Sanyal, offg. Sub Naib Ahilkar	51	45	11	34	——	——	24.44	
Partha Chander Mitter, offg. Sub Naib Ahilkar	66	83	7	57	——	19	10.23	
Sub -Division Mathabhanga								
Sita Nath Banerjee, Naib Ahilkar	249	172	107	56	3	6	65.64	
Ashutosh Ghosh, offg. Sub Naib Ahilkar	106	79	50	29	——	——	63.29	
Harendra Narayan Chowdhuri, Sub Naib Ahilkar	43	49	24	23	2	——	51.06	
Sub Division Mekhliganj								
Moulvie Yajuinudin Ahmed, offg. Naib Ahilkar								
Surapati Chatterjee, Naib Ahilkar	96	78	54	24	——	——	69.23	
	262	147	72	70	2	3	50.70	
TOTAL	26729	1883	923	827	11	122	52.74	

to the Court of Sessions :[98]

There were 19 applications, including 1 pending from

Name of committing Officers	No. of cases	No. of persons committed	No. of persons convicted	No. of persons released	Otherwise disposed of	Remaining pending	Percentage of convictions
Pria Nath Dutt, Fouzdari Ahilkar, Sudder	9	16	10	5	—	1	66.66
Sarapati chatterjee, Naib Ahilkar, Dinhata	2	5	2	3	—	—	40.00
Rameshwar Pramanik, Naib Ahilkar							
Sita Nath Banerjee, Naib Ahilkar,	1	1	—	—	—	1	—
Mathabhanga	6	26	18	8	—	—	69.23
Moulvie Yajuinniddin Ahmed,							
Mekhligunj	1	1	—	1	—	—	—
Sarapati Chatterjee, Naib Ahilkar							
	2	9	—	—	—	9	—
TOTAL	21	58	30	17	—	11	63.82

NAMES OF COURT	Longest period of detention		Shorted period of detention		Average period detention		Remarks
Session Court	Mths	Days	Moths	Days	Moths	Days	
Priya Nath Dutt, M.A., Fouzdari Ahilkar	6	9	-------	9	-------	81	
Harendra Narayan chowdhuri, offg., Sudder	4	20	-------	1	-------	17	
Sub Naib Ahilkar							
Satish Chandra Mustafi, Sub Naib Ahilkar	• 14		-------	1	-------	5	
Yajuinuddin Ahemed, offg. Sudder Sub Naib	• —		-------	1	--------	7	
Ahilkar							
Naib Ahilkar Dinhata (Jogendra Nath Sanyal			-------	1	——	15	
and Purno Chander Mitter)	• 20		-------	1	——	13	
Sita Nath Banerjee, Naib Ahilkar	-----	298	-------	1	-------	3	
Mathabhanga	-----	12					
Harendra Narayan chowdhuri, Sub Naib			------	5	——	22	
Ahilkar, Mathabhanga	• 1						
Ashutosh Ghosh, offg. Sub Naib Ahilkar,			-------	1	——	5	
Ditto							
Sarapati Chatterjee, Naib Ahilkar, Mekhligunj	-----	16	-------	11	——	18	
			-------	1	——	52	
	-----	28					
	5	11					

the previous year, for maintenance against 15 of the previous year; of these 1 was disposed of in favour of the applicant, 13 were dismissed and 4 rejected or struck off and one compromised. Rs. 5 were awarded as compensation to defendant under Section 250 of the Criminal Procedure Code against Rs. 9 awarded during the presiding year. There were 24 cases including 8 pending from the previous year regarding right of way against 21 cases of the previous year. Of these 2 were disposed of in favour of the applications, 7 dismissed, 8 compromised and 7 rejected or struck off.

The appended table shows the result of fine operations during the year under record as compared with the preceding year:[99]

Year	Balance of the previous year	Imposed during the year	Total amount to be released	Released during the year	Remitted of written off	Balance at the end of the year
	Rs. A. P.	Rs. A. P.	Rs. A. P.	Rs. A. P.	Rs. A. P.	Rs. A. P.
1890-91	3,400 11 0	4,688 6 0	8,039 4 0	1,059 6 3	390 0 9	3,539 13 0
1891-92	3,539 13 0	4,699 3 6	8,239 0 0	3,914 15 3	919 2 0	3,101 14 9

92 was Rs. 4,699 – 3 against Rs. 4,688 – 6 and the amount released Rs. 3,919 – 15 – 3 against Rs. 4,059 – 6 – 3 of the previous year. The outstanding balance at the close of the year was Rs. 3,104 – 14 – 9. This was one of the most satisfactory and hoped that the officers, responsible for the realisation of the fines, try their utmost to realize outstandin s or had them written off, where there was no prospect of the realizing the same. The foolowing table exposes the value of stamps and court-fees filed in the different Criminal Courts during the year under report:[100]

Name of Courts	Stamps			Court -fees			Total		
Sudder Criminal Court	643	0	0	1,401	4	0	1,744	4	0
Dinhata ditto	383	8	0	329	0	0	717	8	0
Mathabhanga ditto	510	15	6	358	12	0	869	11	6
Mekhligunj ditto	320	8	0	241	4	0	561	12	0
TOTAL	1,862	16	6	2,030	4	0	3,893	3	6

witness and accused) was 7,758 against 7,736 of the previous year. The following table of miscellaneous work done by the different Criminal Courts:[101]

Names of Court	No. of petitions received	No. of order passed	No. of processes of all kinds issued	No or reports heard	No. of Robocaries received	No. of ball-bonds examined	No. of recognizence	No. of Robocaries issued
Sudder Fouzdari Court	971	987	2326	664	338	393	815	108
Dinhata Court	349	548	2671	328	179	104	348	32
Mathabahnga Court	442	461	2771	583	62	62	336	164
Mekhligunj Court	414	221	1018	256	43	38	164	31

Regarding the charge of the office of Criminal adminstration rested with Babu Priya Nath Dutt, Fouzdari Ahilkar throughout the year (1895 -96) except from the 13th of May to the 4th July, during which period he officiated as Civil and Session Judge and Babu Rajkrishna Das Mookherjee, M.A.,B.L., Assistant Civil Judge was in charge. Babu Rajkrishna Das, officiating Malcutchary Naib Ahilkar and Treasury Officer, tried criminal cases with powers of a second Class Magistrate throughout the year. Babu Jadu nath Bhattacharjee, B.A.,B.L., worked as Sudder Sub Naib Ahilkar throughout the year except from the 11th October to the 25th of November when he was on privilege leave. He resigned his office on the 31st of March with effect from the 1st of April of the current year. Babu Manmohan Buxi, Honorary Magistrate, tried Municipal cases under the Cooch Behar Town Committee Act throughout the year.[102]

Babu Sita Nath Banerjee, Naib Ahilkar was in –charge

of the Sub-division and he was assisted by Sub – Naib Ahilkar Babu Bama Charan Neogi, B.A,B.L., throughout the year except for 10 days from the 26th of February, when he was transferred to Mekhligunj to relieve Babu Ashutosh Ghosh during his illness.[103]

Babu Gopal Chandra Chatterjee, B.A.,B.L.,Naib Ahilkar, remained in charge of the Sub-division throughout the year (1896). He was assisted by Sub Naib Ahilkar Babu Padma Nath Das, B.A,B.L, throughout the year except for 10 days from the 26th February, when he was transferred to Mekhligunj to relieve Babu Ashutosh Ghosh during his illness.[104]

Babu Ashutosh Ghosh on the other hand was in charge of the Sub division throughout the year except for 10 days from 26 the to February to 6th of March when he was ill and Babu Padma Nath Das, Sub- Naib Ahilkar of Mathabhanga was placed in charge.[105]

The following table shows the number of cognizable and non-cognizable cases reported during the past three years :[106]

YEAR	*OFFENCES*		*TOTAL*
	Cognizable	*Non – cognizable*	
1893 – 94	1,281	1,209	2,490
1894 – 95	1,250	1,185	2,435
1895 – 96	1,121	1,331	2,452

These figures shows that cognizable cases decreased by 129, while non-cognizable cases increased by 146. The decrease in cognizable cases is not satisfactorily explained. It is entirely in classes V and VI, i.e. in petty cases, the more serious cases is mostly due to the increase in cases relating to public and local nuisances, offences relating to marriage and offences under local and special Acts. The following statement was a brief analysis of the offences under each classes:[107]

Class I, "Offences against the State, public tranquillity, safety and justice" 43 cases were reported against 25, showing an increase of 18 cases. There were 33 cases of unlawful assembly and rioting against 20 of the previous year. Such an increase in rioting is not creditable to the Police who failed to take any preventive measures or to have any of the parties bound down before –hand to keep the peace. There were also 4 cases relating to coin, stamps, and Government notes against 1 of the previous year.

In Class II, "serious offences against the person", there were 84 cases against 60, showing an increase of 24 cases. The details of the most serious cases under this class are as follows :

There were 2 cases of murder, 2 of culpable homicide, 6 of rape, 9 of kidnapping and 1 of unnatural offence; against 3 cases of murder, 2 of culpable homicide, 2 of rape, 8 of kidnapping and 2 of unnatural offence of the year preceding.

In Class III, "serious offences against property", the offences numbered 368 against 341, showing an increase of 27 cases.

In Class IV, "minor offences against the person", the number was 40 against 27, showing an increase of 13 cases.

In Class V, "minor offences against property", there was a decrease of 170 cases, the number being 536 against 706 of the previous year.

In Class VI, "other offences not specified above", there were 50 cases against 91 of the previous year, showing a decrease of 41 cases.

Statement A, Part II, shows the number of cases &c. In each class non –cognizable offences.

In Class I, "offences against the State, public tranquillity &c.", there were 36 cases against 52 in the year preceding, showing a decrease of 16 cases.

In Class II, "Serious offences against the person", none in the preceding year.

In Class III, " Serious offence against property" there were 21 cases against 13 in the previous year.

In Class IV, "minor offence against the person" there

was an increase of 28 cases, the number being 555 against 527.

In Class V, "minor offence against property", there were 274 cases against 271, showing an increase of 3 cases.

In Class VI, "Other offence not specified above", there were 295 cases against 231, showing an increase of 64 cases.

The cases under special laws were 149 against 91, showing an increase of 58 cases.

The following table shows the number of cases reported and the number of persons brought to trial in all courts during the past and the preceding year :[108]

	1894 - 95	*1895 - 96*
No. of Cognizable and Non-cognizable cases reported	2,435	2,452
Number of persons brought to trial	1,623	1,509
Convicted	751	804
Released	769	596
Otherwise disposed of	10	4
Remaining pending at the ned of the year	93	105
Percentage of persons convicted to total number tried	49.40	57.42

The above figure shows a decrease of 114 persons brought to trial during the year, while the percentage of convictions rose from 49.40 to 57.42. Such a result satisfactory. One hundred five persons in 49 cases were pending trial on the 31st march against 93 persons in 58 cases of the preceding year. Of these persons 1 was pending trial before the Session Judge, 5 before the Fouzdari Ahilkar, 31 before Babu Rajkrishna Das, 47 before Babu Jadu Nath Bhattacharjee, 3 before Babu Sita Nath Banerjee, 8 before Babu Bama Charan Neogi, 1 before Babu Gopal Chander Chatterjee, 1 before Babu Padma Nath Das and 8 before Babu Ashutosh Ghosh. The large number of persons (83) pending trial in the Sudder Sub Division is the most noticeable feature of the above figures.

The number of cases not enquired into under section 157, clause (b), Criminal Procedure Code, was 37 against 102 in the preceeding year.The following table shows the details of the number of persons brought to trial in all courts in cognizable and non –cognizable cases during the year as compared with the preceeding year :[109]

DETAILS	*1894 – 95*		*1895 – 96*	
	Cognizable	*Non-Cognizable*	*Cognizable*	*Non-Cognizable*
Cases reported	1,250	1,185	1,121	1,331
No. of persons brought to trial	920	703	711	798
Convicted	456	295	374	430
Released	398	371	72	324
Otherwise disposed of	8	2	3	1
Remaining under trial at the close of the year	58	35	6	43
Percentage of person convicted to total number trial	53.39	44.29	57.89	57.0

The percentage of convictions in cognizable and non-cognizable cases rose from 53.39 and 44.29 and 44.29 to 57.89 and 57.02 respectively.

Regarding appeals, there were 76 appeals preferred, against the same number to the previous year. Of this 76, 22 were heard by the Judge and 54 by the Fouzdari Ahilkar for the time being. In 55 cases the orders of the Lower Courts were confirmed, in 4 modified and in 15 reversed. The result is not so good as the last year. The following table shows the number of persons convicted and appeals preferred with the result in the case of each officer separately :[110]

The following table shows the longest, shortest and

NAME OF OFFICER	Total number of persons punished	Total number of appeals	Order confirmed	Appeal rejected	Order modified	Order reversed	Pending
Priya Nath Dutt, Fouzdari Ahilkar	61	6	6	-------	-------	------	-------
Hari Das Mukherjee, offg. Ditto							
Sita Nath Banerjee, Naib Ahilkar Dinhata	120	16	7	2	------	7	------
Rajkrishna Das ditto, Sudder	119	13	12	-------	------	1	------
Jadu Nath Bhattacharjee, Sudder Sub Naib Ahilkar	124	8	6	-------	1	1	------
Bama Charan Neogi, Sub Naib Ahilkar Dinhata	54	3	2	-------	------	1	------
Gopal Chandra Chatterjee, Naib Ahilkar Mathabhanga	99	15	12	------	3	------	------
Padma Nath Das, ditto	35	3	2	-------	------	1	------
Asutosh Ghosh, Naib Ahilkar, Mekhligunj	103	12	8	-------	------	4	------
TOTAL	715	76	55	2	4	15	

The following table gives the result of commitments to the Court of Sessions :[111]

Names of Committing Officers	No. of cases	No. of persons committed	No. of persons convicted	No. of persons released	Otherwise disposed of	Remembering pending	Percentage of conviction
PriyaNath Dutt, Fouzdari Ahilkar	7	8	6	2	--------	------	75.00
Sita Nath Banerjee, Naib Ahilkar Dinhata	2	2	------	1	-------	1	-------
Gopal Chander Chatterjee, Naib Ahilkar, Mathabhanga	2	2	2	-------	--------	------	100.00
Ashutosh Ghosh, Naib Ahilkar, Mekhligunj	5	9	3	6	--------	-------	33.33
TOTAL	16	21	11	9	-----	1	55.00

average periods of detention of prisoners pending trial before each court :[112]

Names of Court *detention*	*Longest period of detention*	*Shoertest period of detention*	*Average period of*	*REMARKS*
	Days	Days	Days	It is impossible to believe
Jadab Chander Chakraborty, Session Judge				the figures reported for Babu Jadu Nath
Priya Nath Dutt, Fouzdari Ahilkar	69	9	29.70	Bhattacharjee in the face of the large
Hari Das Mukherjee, offg. Ditto	33	1	9.48	number of pending cases always on his
Raj Krishna Das, Naib Ahilkar Sudder	89	1	14.40	file and the figures given in .....
Jadu nath Bhattacharjee, Sudder Sub – Naib Ahilkar Dinhata	11	1	3.67	
Sita Nath Banerjee, Naib Ahilkar	82	1	13.64	
Bama Charan Neogi, Sub Naib Ahilkar Mathabhanga	30	1	10.36	
Gopal Chandra Chatterjee, Naib Ahilkar	69	1	15.90	
Padma Nath Das, Sub – Naib Ahilkar Mekhligunj	32	2	12.3	
Ashutosh Ghosh, Naib Ahilkar		68	1	16.27

Along with this, there were 12 applications for maintenance against 24 in the preceeding year. Of these 2 were disposed of in favour of applicants, 5 were dismissed and 3 rejected or struck off. 2 remianed pending at the end of the year. Rs. 30 were awarded as compensation to defendants under Section 250 C.P.C. There were 37 cases respecting right of way during the year including 2 pending from the previous year. Of these 3 were disposed of in favour of applicants, 4 dismissed, 15 compromised, 8 rejected or struck off and 2 remained pending at the close of the year.

As detailed below, there were 156 accidental deaths reported during the year against 137 reported during the year previous :[113]

By suicide	3
By drowning	73
By snake bite	41
By wild beast	32
Total	156 deaths

The following table shows the result of operations for realization of fines during the year as compared with the preceding year :[114]

YEAR	Balance of the previous year			Imposed during the year			Total amount to be released			Released during the year			Remitted or written off			Balance at the end of the year		
	Rs.	A.	P.	Rs.	A.	P.	Rs.	A.	P.	Rs.	A.	P.	Rs.	A.	P.	Rs.	A.	P.
1894–95	1,225	15	6	4,070	12	9	5,296	12	3	3,596	12	3	240	0	0	1,460	0	0
1895–96	1,460	0	0	4,098	15	6	5,558	15	6	3,887	12	0	859	11	9	811	7	9

The amount released was Rs. 3,887 -12 – 0 against Rs. 3,596 -12 – 3 and the amount written off was also greater than in the previous year with the result that the outstanding balance at the close of the year was reduced from Rs. 1,460 to 811 – 7 – 9. The percentage of realizations to fines imposed during the year is 94.6, which was good one. The following table shows the value of Stamps and Court fees filed in the different Courts during the year :[115]

Name of Courts	Stamps			Court-fees			Total		
	Rs.	A.	P.	Rs.	A.	P.	Rs.	A.	P.
Sudder Criminal Courts	975	0	0	955	8	0	1,930	8	0
Dinhata ditto	622	8	0	346	4	0	968	12	0
Mathabhanga ditto	397	11	9	374	4	0	771	15	9
Mekhligunj ditto	443	0	0	327	0	0	770	0	0

The following annexed statement shows the number and detention of witness who appeared before the different Criminal Courts in cases entered in Register, in cases in which the defendants appeared.

					One day	Two days	Three days	Four days	Five or seven days	REMARKS
1	2	3	4	5	6	7	8	9	10	11
Priya Nath Dutt, Fouzdari Ahilkar										
Hari Das Mukherjee, Offg. Fouzdari Ahilkar	655	626	29	-----	615	34	6	----	----	
Raj Krishna Das, Naib Ahilkar	568	568	------	-----	540	24	4	---	----	
Jadu Nath Bhattacherjee, Sudder	401	363	29	9	328	41	23	----	---	
Sub Naib Ahilkar	11	11	------	-----	11	----	---	----	----	
Mon Mohon Baxi, Honorary Magistrate Dinhata	996	870	126		720	200	57	19	----	
Sita Nath Banerjee, Naib Ahilkar				-----						
Bama Charan Neogi, Sub Naib Ahilkar	583	485	98		400	114	51	6	12	
Mathabhanga	387	376	11	-----	375	12	---	----	----	
Gopal Chandra Chatterjee, Naib Ahilkar				-----						
Padma Nath Das, Sub Naib Ahilkar	137	136	1		126	11	---	----	----	
Mekhl;igunj				-----						
Ashutosh Ghosh, Naib Ahilkar	652	618	34	-----	475	135	32	5	5	
TOTAL	4,390	4,053	328	9	3,590	571	173	30	17	

The following statement shows the number and detention of witnesses who appeared before the different Criminal Courts in cases entered in Register :[116]

Name of Officers	Total number of witnesses that appeared	No. of witnesses examined	No. of witnesses discharged without examination	No. of witnesses not examined and finally discharged	Detention of witness entered in columns 3 and 4					
					One day	Two days	Three days	Four days	Five or seven days	REMARKS
1	2	3	4	5	6	7	8	9	10	11
Priya Nath Dutt, Fouzdari Ahilkar										
Hari Das Mukherjee, Offg. Fouzdari Ahilkar	249	249	----	-----	249	----	----	----	-----	
Raj Krishna Das, Naib Ahilkar	117	117	-----	-----	117	---	----	---	-----	
Jadu Nath Bhattacherjee, Sudder Sub Naib Ahilkar	27	22	5	---	27	---	----	----	---	
	------	-----	------	---	----	-----	---	-----	----	

Mon Mohon Baxi, Honorary Magistrate Dinhata	336	309	27	----	221	95	10	10	---	
Sita Nath Banerjee, Naib Ahilkar	23	22	1	----	20	1	2	2	---	
Bama Charan Neogi, Sub Naib Ahilkar Mathabhanga	369	336	33	----	339	30	---	---	---	
Gopal Chandra Chatterjee, Naib Ahilkar	226	221	5	----	220	6	---	---	----	
Padma Nath Das, Sub Naib Ahilkar Mekhl;igunj	527	448	79	----	425	102	---	---	---	
Ashutosh Ghosh, Naib Ahilkar										
TOTAL	1,874	1,724	150	----	1,618	234	12	10	---	
Grand Total of Witnesses in both C and A Register case.	6,264	5,777	478	9	5,208	805	185	40	17	

The number of witness who appeared before the different Criminal Courts during the year was 6264 against 6655. Of these, 5777 witnesses were examined, 478 discharged without examination and 9 witnesses remained to be examined at the end of the year, aginst 5767, 919 and 79 respectively of the previous year. Only 17 witnesses were unavoidably detained for five to seven days.

The following statement shows the miscellaneous work done by the different Criminal Courts :[117]

Names of Court	No. Of petitioners received	No. of processes of all kinds issued	No. of reports heard	No. of Robocaries received	No. of ball-bonds executed	No. of recognizence	No. of robocaries issued
Sudder Fouzdari Court	1,396	3,940	917	350	321	500	28
Dinhata Court	750	3,049	142	54	81	362	50
Mathabhnaga Court	354	3,157	299	51	67	127	120
Mekhligunj Court	430	2,618	336	80	74	222	70
TOTAL	2,930	12,764	1,694	535	545	1,211	268

Regarding village chowkidars during the year was 1590 against 1580, shows an increase of 10 Chowkidars. The number of Chowkidars in each Sub – division is shown below :[118]

Sub–division	*Chowkidars*
Sudder	529
Dinhata	380
Mathabhanga	461
Mekhligunj	220
Total	1,530

The number of petitions received from Chowkidars requisting that their arrear pay should be realized was 1127 against 1037 showing an increase of 90 petitions.

The following statement shows the amount realized in each sub–division :[119]

Sub–division	*Amounts realized*		
	Rs.	*A*	*P*
Sudder	2,357	7	0
Dinhata	796	6	6
Mathabhanga	1,773	11	9
Mekhligunj	542	15	9
TOTAL	5,470	9	0

Of this amount, Rs. 5,295 – 0 – 3 were paid to the Chowkidars and the balance Rs. 175 – 8 – 9 remained to be paid at the end of the year.

The annexed statement shows the working of the village Chowkidari fund during the year:[120] (see facing page)

The total amount of deductions from the chowkidars pay including fines and penalties realized during the year, amounted to Rs. 6,134 – 14 – 9 .

The Fouzdari Ahilkar was out on tour for 56 days and inspected the Sub –divisional courts, offices and Lock –ups. He also inspected most of the out –posts, pounds, hats and Bundars and inquired about the working of the chowkidari system, crime, bad characters, prospects of crops and the condition of the people.

The number of days passed on tour by each Sub – divisional officer is shown below :[121]

Sita Nath Banerjee, Naib Ahilkar, Dinhata	43 days	
Bama Charan Neogi, Sub Naib Ahilkar, Dinhata	15 days	58
Gopal Chander Chatterjee, Naib Ahilkar, Mathabhanga	48 days	
Padma Nath Das, Sub –Naib Ahilkar	60 days	108
Ashutosh Ghosh, Naib Ahilkar, Mekhligunj	47 days	
Padma Nath Das —— ditto	2 days	49

In 1896 – 97 Priya Nath Dutt, M.A, B.L., was Fouzdari Ahilkar throughout the year but was on privilege leave from the 21st of November 1897 to the 6th of February 1898, during which period Babu Narendra Nath Sen, B.L.,

Names of sub divisions	Total amount of annual fund deductions	Balance of the provisions year	Total	Amount realized during the year	Amount remained unrealised on the 31st March	Amount of fines realized	Amount of penalties realized	Miscellaneous receipts	Total of columns 5,7, 8, & 9
1	2	3	4	5	6	7	8	9	10
Sudder	1,740 2 0	622 12 0	2362 14 0	14967 9	866 6 3	87 14 0	180 3 0	1 4 0	1765 12 9
Dinhata	1,301 0 0	718 1 3	2019 1 3	777 9 0	1241 8 3	56 14 9	26 9 0	2 6 0	863 6 9
Mathabhanga	1,764 6 0	487 15 11	2252 5 11	1839 2 0	374 3 0	366 0 0	153 3 6	------	2358 5 6
Mekhligunj	834 10 9	477 6 3	1312 1 0	1011 1 9	300 15 3	126 15 6	9 4 6	------	1147 5 9
Total	5640 2 9	2306 3 5	7946 6 2	5121 4 6	2783 0 0	637 12 3	367 4 0	3 10 0	6134 14 9

Assistant Civil Judge, officiated for him. The names of the officers who held charge of the subordinate criminal posts and the changes which took place, shows in the following statements :[121]

Sub - Division	Name of Naib Ahilkar	Term Employed	Name of Sub Naib Ahilkar	Term employed
Sudder -------------	Babu Gopal Chandra Chatterjee	1st April 1897 to 8th February 1898	Babu Pramatha Nath Chatterjee, M.A., B.L.	1st March to 31st March 1898
	Babu Raj Krishna Das	9th February to 31st March 1898		
Tufangunj ----------	Baba Harendra Narayan Chowdhury, B.L	1st April 1897 to 6th February 1898	Babu Bama Charan Neogi, B.L.	1st April to 6th February 1898
	Bama Charan Neogi, B.L.	7th February to 31st March 1898		
Dinhata --------------	Baba Hari Nath Basu, B.L.	1st April 1897 to 31st March 1898	Babu Rajani Kanta Bhoumik, M.A., B.L.	1st to 7th April 1897 and from 14th May 1897 to 31st March 1898.
Mathabhanga -------	Babu Ashutosh Ghosh, B.L.	1st April to 30th May 1897 and from 30th June 1897 to 31st March 1898.	Babu Surendra Nath Chakerbutty, M.A. B.L.	8th April to 12th May 1897
			Babu Jagad Ballabh Biswas, M.A., B.L.	1st April 1897 to 30th May 1897 and 30th June 1897 to 31st March 1898
	Jagad Ballabh Biswas, M.A., B.L.	31st May to 29th June 1897.		
Mekhligunj ----------	Babu Padma Nath Das, B.L.	1st April 1897 to 31st March 1898	N I L	NIL

Municipal cases in the town of Cooch Behar were tried by Babu Mon Mohan Buxi. There was no change in the personnel of the officers during the year under report.

The number of cases instituted in the past three years were as follows :[122]

YEAR	*OFFENCE*		*Total*
	Cognizable	*Non-Cognizable*	
1895 – 96	1,121	1,331	2,452
1896 – 97	1,265	1,264	2,529
1897 – 98	1,253	1,144	2,397

The decrease in cognizable cases is 12 only and calls for no explanation. The decrease of 120 non –cognizable cases is attributed partly to the people having less surplus money to spend on litigation owing to the high prices, but briefly owing to the effect of the earthquake which seemed to paralyze the people and chain them to their homes; so that, although the courts were open and ready to work within 4 days of the earthquake, the litigants refused to come to court and even when they came objected to enter the court house from fear of its collapse should another earthquake take place.

Analysis of cognizable crime —— Statement A, Parts I & III :[123]

Class I.— The return shows a decrease of 3 cases under this class, the figures being 44 against 47 in the previous year. No less than 40 of these cases were under the hearing of rioting. This is due to the occurrence of several causes of grain riots and it was beyond the power of the Police to prevent most of these cases.

Class II. —— 109 cases were reported against 96 in the previous year or an increase of 13 cases. The chief increase in under kidnapping 24 cases against 18 and grievous hurt, 30 against 17. There were also 3 cases of capable homicide against 2 in 1896 -97. There were only 2 cases of murder against 7 in the previous year.

Class III. ——— There is a satisfactory decrease of 89 cases, the number being 343 against 432. The decrease is under lurking house trespass under which the number of cases has gone down from 401 to 299. Last year the number rose owing to the high prices of grain. In the year under report high prices ruled for 3 months only and they affected crime for only 2 months and 12 days or up to the date of the earthquake. The figures of the year under this class are less than those of 1895 – 96 by 23 cases.

Class IV.——— There is a decrease of 7 cases, the figures being 43 against 50. The fluctuation calls for no remark.

Class V. ——— The decrease under Class III is to some extent counterbalanced by an increase of 59 cases, the number being 658 against 599. The increase is under theft where the figures went up from 371 to 472.

Class VI. ——— There were 56 cases against 41 showing an increase of 15 cases. There were 6 more cases under Vagrancy, 5 more under the Arms Act, 3 under the Gambling Act and 6 under "other laws" balanced by small reduction under other headings, the largest being 7 cases under excise.

Analysis of non–cognizable crime ——— Statement B:[124]

Class I. ——— The number of cases went down from 70 to 54. There were only 33 offences against public justice and 10 of false evidence against 43 and 17. There were slight increase under other headings.

Class II. —— Is blank against one case last year.

Class III. —— Shows 9 cases against 13 in 1896 -97.

Class IV. ——— The number of cases has gone up from 510 to 575 or by 65 cases of criminal force have increased from 319 to 380 or by 61 and there is also an increase of 6 hurt cases.

Class V. ——— There is a decrease of 60 cases, the total being 215 against 275. There is a decrease of 44 cases of mischief and 17 of criminal misappropriation.

Class IV. ———— The figures are 219 against 249 or a decrease of 30 cases, chiefly under intimidation, 23 and public and local nuisances, 7. The other fluctuations are small and balance each other.

The number of cases has gone down from 146 to 123 or by 23 cases. The number of cases under the Cooch

Behar Town Committee Act decreased from 70 to 48 or by 22 cases. The other fluctuations are petty and nearly balance each other.

There were two following tables compares the results of trial as regards persons for the past two years. In the first totals are given, and in the second these totals are distributed between cognizable and non–cognizable cases:[125]

Particulars	*1896–97*	*1897–98*
Number of cognizable and non–cognizable cases reported	2,529	2,397
Number of persons brought to trial	1,402	1,839
Convicted	759	1,038
Released	579	735
Otherwise disposed of	2	2
Pending at the end of the year	62	64
Percentage of persons convicted to total number tried	56.64	58.47

Details	*1896 – 97*		*1897 – 98*	
	Cognizable	*Non-cognizable*	*Cognizable*	*Non-cognizable*
Cases Reported	1,265	1,264	1,253	1,144
Number of persons brought to trial	720	682	977	862
Convicted	406	353	598	440
Released	277	302	337	398
Otherwise disposed of	0	2	2	———
Pending at the end of the year	37	25	40	24
Percentage of number convicted to total number tried	59.44	53.7	63.82	52.50

The number of persons brought to trial has increased notwithstanding the decrease in the number of cases. This is due partly to the fact that a large number of persons were sent up in some causes of theft of grain with riot, but it is also due partly to the decreased number of accused who were summoned as witnesses. Bad habits die hard, and regret that cases such as those described earlier still recur though were much decreased. The percentage of convictions in Police cases has risen from 59.44 to 63.82, which was good but the result, greatly due to the grain cases mentioned above. The percentage in non –cognizable cases has gone down from 53.72 to 52.50. This was to be expected owing to the restriction placed on the summoning of defendants as witnesses. The number of persons pending trial was not excessive. This will be dealt with hereafter.

The Police refused to enquire into 54 cases as against 48 in the previous year. The figures call for no remark.

One of the two cases of murder was reported as false. In the other case a man went to fetch his young wife from her home. She refused to go with him so he cut her throat. He was sentenced to transportation for life. One of the three cases of capable homicide not amounting to murder was pending at the close of the year. The other two cases both arose from land disputes. One man was killed in each case and both ended in conviction, five persons being convicted in one case and four in the other and sentenced to various terms of imprisonment. One of the two cases of dacoity was reported as false. In the other the Police sent up 16 persons of whom the Fouzdari Ahilkar discharged 5 and committed 11, who were pending trial at the end of the year, and have since been acquitted. The property taken in this case was valued at Rs. 1,455 – 9 – 6. None of the other cases are of public interest.

The number of appeals and their result are shown ahead:[126] (see facing page)

Of the above 16 were heard by the Judge and the rest by the Fouzdari Ahilkar. There were few reversals and the results were on the whole satisfactory one. The percentage of appeals to persons convicted in appealable cases is almost the same as the last year viz 9.8 against 9.7.

The following table ahead shows the distribution of

Name of the officers	Total No. of persons punished	Total number of appeals	Order confirmed	Appeal rejected	Order modified	Pending
Babu Priya Nath Dutt, Fouzdary Ahilkar	62	10	8	1	——	——
Narendra Nath Sen, ditto	17	6	3	1	——	——
Gopal Chandra Chaterjee, Sudder Naib Ahilkar	160	7	4	1	——	——
Raj Krishna Das, Sudder offg. Naib Ahilkar	31	2	2	——	——	——
Harendra Narayan Chowdhuri, Naib Ahilkar, Tufangunj	87	2	1	——	——	——
Bama Charan Neogi, Addl.,Sub Naib Ahilkar, ditto	6	2	1	——	1	——
Bama Charan Neogi, Sub Naib Ahilkar, ditto	40	4	4	——	——	——
Hari Nath Basu, Naib Ahilkar, Dinhata	119	12	12	1	1	——
Rajani Kanta Bhowmik, Sub Naib Ahilkar, Mathabhanga	87	11	11	1	——	——
Ashutosh Ghosh, Naib Ahilkar , Mathabhanga	197	17	17	1	3	——
Jagad Ballabh Biswas, Sub Naib Ahilkar, Mathabhanga	68	7	7	——	1	——
Padma Nath Das, Naib Ahilkar, Mekhligunj	85	14	14	——	2	——
TOTAL ——————	957	94	65	6	8	——

Names of Officers	No. of cases	No. of persons under trial	Convicted	Acquitted or discharged	Otherwise disposed off	Remaining pending trial at the close of the year	Percentage of conviction to total number tried	Remarks
Sudder								
Jadab Chandra Chakraborty, Session Judge	15	49	20	18	-----	11	52.63	
Priya Nath Dutta, Fouzdari Ahilkar	220	138	62	71	-----	5	46.61	
Narendra Nath Sen, offg.,Fouzdari Ahilkar	71	42	17	25	-----	-----	40.47	
Gopal Chandra Chatterjee, Naib Ahilkar	384	268	160	108	-----	-----	59.70	
Raj Krishna Das, naib Ahilkar	84	46	31	12	-----	3	72.09	
Pramath Nath Chatterjee, Sub Naib Ahilkar	38	18	8	4	-----	6	66.6	
Munmohan Buxi, Honorary Magistrate	47	47	44	3	-----	-----	93.62	

Sub Division Toofangunj								
Harendra Narayan Chowdhuri, Naib Ahilkar	117	119	87	3	------	------	73.10	
Bama Charan Neogi, Additional Naib Ahilkar	74	45	6	21	-----	18	22.2	
Bama Charan Neogi, Sub Naib Ahilkar	110	94	40	54	------	------	42.50	
Sub Divisiopn Dinhata								
Hari Nath Bose, Naib Ahilkar	301	184	119	65	------	-----	64.67	
Rajani Kanta Bhowmik, Sub Naib Ahilkar	155	120	87	32	------	1	73.10	
Surendra Nath Charabutty, offg. Sub Naib Ahilkar	3	3	1	2	-------	------	33.3	
Sub Division Mathabhanga								
Ashutosh Ghosh , Naib Ahilkar	297	291	195	83	2	11	69.64	
Jagad ballabh Biswas, Offg. Naib Ahilkar,	29	16	7	9	-------	------	43.75	
Jagad Ballabh Biswas, Sub Naib Ahilkar	154	191	68	121	------	2	35.96	
Sub Division Mekhligunj								
Padma Nath Das, Naib Ahilkar	399	168	86	75	-------	7	53.41	
Total	2,498	1,839	1,038	735	2	64	58.47	

work and the percentage of convictions before each other:[127]

The Percentage of convictions was higher than in the previous year being 52.63 against 37.03. It is unfair to judge an officer's work by the result of so small a number of cases as were ordinarily committed by a single officer. Since the close of the year the 11 persons shown as pending have been acquitted which will reduce the percentage to

Names of committing Officers	No. of cases	No. of persons committed	No. of persons convicted	No. of persons released	Otherwise disposed of	Remaining pending	Percentage of convicted
Priya Nath Dutt, Fouzdari Ahilkar	2	12	-------	1	-------	11	-------
Narendra Nath Sen, Offg. Fouzdari Ahilkar	1	5	5	-------	------	------	100
Harendra Nath Chowdhuri, Naib Ahilkar, Toofangunj	1	1	------	1	-------	------	-----
Hari Nath Bose, Naib Ahilkar, Dinhata	2	6	6	-------	-------	-------	100
Ashutosh Ghosh, Naib Ahilkar, Mathabhanga	3	6	1	5	------	------	16.6
Padma Nath Das, Naib Ahilkar, Mekhligunj	6	19	8	11	------	------	42.10
	15	49	20	18	------	11	52.63

Period of detention of prisoners, the usual table is

Name of officers	Longest period of detention	Shortest Period of detention	Average period of detention	Remark
Sudder	Days.	Days.	Days.	
Jadab Chandra Chakraborty, Session Judge	38	1	25.97	
Priya Nath Dutta, Fouzdari Ahilkar	29	1	8.14	
Narendra Nath sen, offg. Fouzdari Ahilkar	20	1	7.8	
Gopal Chandra Chatterjee, Sudder Naib Ahilkar	27	1	9.22	
Raj Krishna Das, Sudder Naib Ahilkar	21	7	10.57	
Pramatha Nath Chatterjee, Sudder Sub Naib Ahilkar	6	--------	6	

Toofangunj				
Harendra Narayan Chowdhuri, Naib Ahilkar	109	1	30.30	
Bama Charan Neogi, Additional Naib Ahilkar	79	1	22.91	
Bama Charan Neogi, Sub Naib Ahilkar	15	3	13.33	
Dinhata				
Hari Nath Bose, Naib Ahilkar, Naib Ahilkar	46	1	11.28	
Rajani kanta Bhowmik, Sub Naib Ahilkar	36	1	10.85	
Mathabhanga				
Ashutosh Ghosh, Naib Ahilkar	29	1	6.82	
Jagad Ballabh Biswas, Sub Naib Ahilkar	44	1	16.77	
Mekhligunj	77	1	12.89	
Padma Nath Das, Naib Ahilkar				

given below :[129]

Miscellaneous proceedings under the code of criminal

Nature of case	No. of cases	Dismissel	Decreed or order passed against the accused	Compromised	Struck off	Pending
Maintenance	12	6	3	1	2	------
Right of way	36	12	11	2	7	4
Security to keep the peace 106,107, 109, & 110, C.P.C	22	8	8	1	------	5

According to record, maintenance cases were more successful than in the previous year, but in only 3 cases were decrees obtained. Under the other headings results are better. Rs. 90 were awarded as compensation under section 250 C.P.C against Rs. 65 of the last year.

But for the eight deaths due to the earthquake the total would have been the same as last year. The actual figures are 160 against 152 devided as shown below :[131]

Suicide	6
Drowning	71
Snake–bite	48
Wild–beast	5
Fall of building	8
Fire	4
All other causes	18
Total	160

YEAR	Balance of the previous year	Imposed during the year	Total amount to be released	Released during the year	Remitted or written off	Balance at the end of the year
	Rs. A. P.	Rs. A. P.	Rs. A. P.	Rs. A. P.	Rs. A. P.	Rs. A. P.
1896–97	811 7 9	4,802 1 0	5,613 8 9	4,689 11 9	117 0 0	806 13 0
1897-98	806 13 0	4,378 9 0	5,185 6 0	4,196 4 6	35 4 0	953 13 6

The percentage of realization to new fines fell from 97.66 to 95.6. The amount of remission is small as the report for remission was received after the close of the

Name of Court	Stamps			Court -fees			Total		
	Rs.	A.	P.	Rs.	A.	P.	Rs.	A.	P.
Sudder Criminal Court	430	3	3	606	4	0	1,036	7	3
Toofangunj Court	235	0	0	155	4	0	390	4	0
Dinhata Court	451	8	0	305	12	0	757	4	0
Mathabahnga Court	535	2	6	402	12	0	937	14	6
Mekhligunj Court	361	0	0	223	4	0	584	4	0

The decrease in non–cognizable cases accounts for the decrease of Rs. 277 – 13. There is a decrease in all the Sub–divisions except Toofangunj and Mathabahnga.

Name and designation of Magistrate	Total number of witness who appeared during the year	No. of witnesses examined	No. of witnessdischarged without examination	No. of witnesses not examined and finally discharged	One days	Two days	Three days	Five days	Five to seven days	Eight or fifteen days	Remarks
1	2	3	4	5	6	7	8	9	10	11	
Sudder											
Priya Nath Dutta, Fouzdari Ahilkar	547	536	11	——	485	61	1	——	——	——	
Narendra Nath Sen, Offg. Fouzdari Ahilkar	154	130	21	——	120	26	8	——	——	——	
Gopal Chandra Chatterjee, Naib Ahilkar	301	301	——	——	283	9	9	——	——	——	
Raj Krishna Das, Naib Ahilkar	158	158	——	——	148	2	8	——	——	——	
Pramath Nath Chatterjee, Sub Naib Ahilkar	57	57	——	——	57	——	——	——	——	——	
Mon Mohun Buxi, Honorary, Magistrate	11	11	——	——	8	——	3	——	——	——	
Total	1,228	1,193	35	——	1101	98	29	——	——	——	

Toofangunj											
Harendra Narayan Chowdhuri	250	204	46	——	138	78	17	17	——	——	
Bama Charan Neogi, Additional Naib Ahilkar	258	195	14	49	148	20	14	27	——	——	
Bama Charan Neogi, Sub Naib Ahilkar	273	236	37	——	138	63	27	32	13	——	
Total	781	635	97	49	424	161	58	76	13	——	
Dinhata											
Hari Nath Bose, Naib Ahilkar	680	538	142	——	429	167	50	26	8	——	
Surendra Nath Chakraborty, Sub Naib Ahilkar	35	31	4	——	33	2	——	——	——	——	
Rajani Kanta Bhowmik, Sub Naib Ahilkar	559	423	136	——	405	117	22	10	5	——	
Total	1,274	992	282	——	867	286	72	36	13	——	
Mathabahnga											
Ashutosh Ghosh, Naib Ahilkar	725	669	56	——	648	57	6	3	11	——	
Jagad Ballabh Biswas, Sub Naib Ahilkar	541	505	36	——	433	74	34	——	——	——	
Total	1,266	1174	92	——	1081	131	40	3	11	——	
Mekhligunj											
Padma Nath Das, naib Ahilkar	766	565	172	29	326	201	124	50	34	2	
Total	5,315	4,559	678	78	3799	877	323	165	71	2	

The following table shows the detention of witnesses:[134]

The result are necessarily worse than last year as only one register had been maintained. There was practically no detention in the Sudder Sub Division and not much in Mathabhanga., but in other three Sub Divisions all show badly in Dinhata only 68 percent of the witness were discharged the first day; Toofangunj 58 percent and in Mekhligunj only 44 per cent. The remark on carelessly prepared returns and the matters has been brought to the notice of the Fouzdari Ahilkar.

The usual return of the miscellaneous work is shown

Names of Courts	No. of petitions received	No. of process ed of all kinds of issues	No. of reports heard	No. of robocar ies receive d	No. of ball-bonds executed	No. of recogniz ances	No. of roboc aries issued
Sudder Fouzdari Court	636	2,566	386	321	99	209	10
Toofangunj Court	290	2,966	125	4	66	197	31
Dinhata Court	640	2,574	185	72	103	218	50
Mathabhanga Court	463	2,992	355	91	78	191	140
Mekhligunj Court	286	1,691	322	60	34	111	24
Total	2,315	12,789	1,373	586	380	932	255

The number of processes issued in Toofangunj is out of all proportion to the number of cases and explanation has been called for. With the reduction in the number of cases there is necessarily a corresponding reduction in the number of processes. The accused in the grain riots were generally kept in Hajat, so the number of bail bonds and recognizance has not increased with the increased number of persons tried.

The number of petitions went down from 83 to 50. In 13 cases the wives were made over to their husbands 28 cases were struck off and 7 were referred to the Civil Court as the women denied the marriage. The remainin g

2 cases were pending.

The number of sub divisions under chowkidars supervision at the close of the year :[136]

Sub Division	*Chowkidars*
Sudder	319
Toofangunj	211
Dinhata	379
Mathabhanga	454
Mekhligunj	216
Total	1,579

The number was 1587 last year. The reduction in the two last named sub divisions is owing to Mathabhanga and Haldibari having been created owns.

The number of the petitions for realization of pay presented by Chowkidars all from 1897 to 1683; a substancial decrease of 214 petitions. The decrease is due to the better condition of the people during the last nine months of the year. The larger realizations are due to the same cause.

Sub Division	*Sum Released in 1896-97*			*Sum Released in 1897-98*		
	Rs.	*A.*	*P.*	*Rs.*	*A.*	*P.*
Sudder	1,870	14	7	2,198	4	9
Toofangunj	649	10	9	771	12	6
Dinhata	1,174	3	6	847	2	3
Mathabhanga	1,850	12	9	1,966	7	3
Mekhligunj	1,003	8	6	1,107	9	0
Total	6,549	2	1	6,891	3	9

The whole of the amount realized was made over to the Chowkidars within the year except Rs. 367 – 9 which remained undisbursed. The financial working of the fund is shown below :[137]

Names of Sub Divisions	Total amount of Annual fund deductions	Balance of the previous year	Total	Amount released during the year	Amount remaind unreleased	Amount remaind unreleased on the 31st March	Amount of fines released	Miscellaneous receipts	Total of columns 5, 7, 8,9.
Sudder	1109 2 6	506 13 0	1615 15 6	957 6 3	658 9 3	176 1 0	165 2 0	10 0 0	1308 9 3
Toofangunj	735 10 5	283 7 9	1019 2 2	588 4 0	430 14 2	20 14 0	75 13 6	--------	684 15 6
Dinhata	1361 8 0	861 2 9	2222 10 9	582 13 0	1639 13 9	15 12 0	70 4 0	--------	668 13 0
Mathabhanga	1744 11 0	432 15 9	2177 10 9	1833 8 3	344 2 6	217 14 0	480 13 6	--------	2538 3 9
Mekhligunj	828 2 6	751 9 0	1579 11 6	719 5 0	830 6 6	99 6 0	135 3 9	1 4 0	985 2 9
Total	5779 2 5	2836 0 3	8613 2 8	1711 4 6	3903 14 2	529 15 0	933 4 9	11 4 0	6185 12 3
1	2	3	4	5	6	7	8	9	10

The Fouzdari Ahilkar reports that the Act, which has now been in force for nearly 5 years, has on the whole worked well. The maximum and minimum pay of the Chowkidars was the same as last year viz Rs. 6 and Rs. 4 – 4 .[138]

Thus the whole system of Criminal justice represents a unique feature of the State of Cooch Behar under the rule of Maharaja Nripendra Narayan. Judicial administration found a stereotype frame under the supervision of the Maharaja in Council.

NOTES AND REFERENCES :

1. Annual Administration Report of the Cooch Behar State (1878 – 79) , p. 33.
2. *Ibid.*
3. *Ibid.*
4. *Ibid.*, p. 34.
5. *Ibid.*
6. *Ibid.*, p. 35.
7. *Ibid.*
8. *Ibid.*
9. *Ibid.*, p. 36.
10. *Ibid.*
11. *Ibid.*
12. *Ibid.*
13. *Ibid.*, p. 37.
14. *Ibid.*
15. *Ibid.*
16. *Ibid.*, p. 38.
17. Annual Administration Report of the Cooch Behar State (1880 -81), p. 28.
18. *Ibid.*, p. 29.
19. *Ibid.*
20. *Ibid.*, p. 30.
21. *Ibid.*
22. *Ibid.*, p. 31.

23. *Ibid*.
24. *Ibid*., p. 32.
25. *Ibid*., p. 33.
26. *Annual Administration Report of the Cooch behar State (1883 -84)*, p. 5.
27. *Ibid*.
28. *Ibid*.
29. *Ibid*., p. 6.
30. *Ibid*.
31. *Ibid*.
32. *Ibid*., p. 7.
33. *Ibid*.
34. *Ibid*.
35. *Ibid*., p. 8.
36. *Ibid*.
37. *Ibid*.
38. *Ibid*., p. 9.
39. *Ibid*.
40. *Ibid*.
41. *Ibid*.
42. *Ibid*.
43. *Ibid*., p. 10.
44. *Ibid*.
45. *Ibid*.
46. *Ibid*., p. 11.
47. *Ibid*.
48. *Ibid*.
49. *Ibid*.
50. *Ibid*.
51. *Ibid*.
52. *Ibid*., p. 12.
53. *Ibid*.
54. *Ibid*.
55. *Ibid*.

56. *Ibid.*, p. 13.
57. *Ibid.*
58. *Ibid.*
59. *Ibid.*
60. Annual Administration Report of the Cooch behar State (1885–86), p. 1.
61. *Ibid.*
62. *Ibid.*
63. *Ibid.*, p. 2.
64. *Ibid.*
65. *Ibid.*
66. *Ibid.*, p. 3
67. *Ibid.*
68. *Ibid.*, p. 4.
69. *Ibid.*
70. *Ibid.*
71. *Ibid.*, p. 5.
72. *Ibid.*
73. *Ibid.*
74. *Ibid.*
75. *Ibid.*
76. *Ibid.*, p. 6.
77. *Ibid.*
78. *Ibid.*, p. 7.
79. *Ibid.*
80. *Ibid.*, p. 8.
81. *Ibid.*
82. *Ibid.*, p. 9.
83. Annual Administration Report of the Cooch Behar State (1891-92), p. 2.
84. *Ibid.*
85. *Ibid.*, p. 3.
86. *Ibid.*
87. *Ibid.*

88. *Ibid*., p. 4.
89. *Ibid*.
90. *Ibid*.
91. *Ibid*., p. 5.
92. *Ibid*.
93. *Ibid*.
94. *Ibid*., p. 6.
95. *Ibid*.
96. *Ibid*.
97. *Ibid*., p. 7.
98. *Ibid*., p. 8.
99. *Ibid*.
100. *Ibid*.
101. *Ibid*., p. 9.
102. Annual Administration Report of the Cooch Behar State (1895-96), p. 22.
103. *Ibid*.
104. *Ibid*., p. 23.
105. *Ibid*.
106. *Ibid*., p. 24.
107. *Ibid*.
108. *Ibid*., p. 25.
109. *Ibid*.
110. *Ibid*., p. 26.
111. *Ibid*.
112. *Ibid*., p. 27.
113. *Ibid*.
114. *Ibid*.
115. *Ibid*., p. 28.
116. *Ibid*.
117. *Ibid*., p. 29.
118. *Ibid*.
119. *Ibid*., p. 30.
120. *Ibid*.

121. *Ibid*., p. 31.
122. *Annual Administration Report of the Cooch Behar State (1897–98)*, p. 2.
123. *Ibid*.
124. *Ibid*., p. 3.
125. *Ibid*.
126. *Ibid*., p. 4.
127. *Ibid*., p. 5.
128. *Ibid*.
129. *Ibid*., p. 6.
130. *loc.cit*.
131. *Ibid*., p. 7.
132. *Ibid*.
133. *Ibid*., p. 8.
134. *Ibid*.
135. *Ibid*., p. 9.
136. *Ibid*.
137. *Ibid*., p. 10.
138. *Ibid*.

3

Law and Order System in Cooch Behar State

The Cooch Behar State Regency Council, during the reign of Maharaja Nripendra Narayan framed an exclusive format of law and order in favour of the State. When Maharaja Nripendra Narayan attained maturity each and every aspect reaches the peak point under his guidance, the department like law and order is not an exception to that. He tried to strengthen the administrative section of the State on the line of European model, which also facilitate his welfare attitude as a monarch. Well developed Law and order also indicate modern outlook of a State.

In 1878 the Police administration has been categories and the cost of maintenance under the following heads:[1]

Strength	Rs.
• Superintendent (1)	5,454
• Inspectors (3)	4,500
• Sub–Inspectors (9)	6,480
• Head Constables (28)	5,280
• Constables (259)	20,436
Total	42,150

The increase under the item of Superintendent's Pay is due to the increments of Rs. 50 to his salary sanctioned two years ago viz, an increase of Rs. 100 in two annual increments of Rs. 50 each. The increase under the head of Sub –inspectors is due to the appointment of an extra Sub–inspector for Huldibari police station, which has been made a thana, in consequence of its increased importance as a railway station on the principal road of the State.

The sub-inspector was appointed in 1878, but paid from savings no provision having been made on the budget for the purpose. The increase in the number of constables and consequent increased cost is due to the appointment of 15 extra constables as guards for the sub –divisional lock-ups.[2]

Formerly the sub-divisional treasure chest, which is kept in the guard house attached to the lock-up and the lock-up itself were under the guard of one sentry only. This man naturally kept watch near the door of the guard house where the treasure was kept. The far side of the lock-up was thus quite unguarded and on stormy nights it was easy for the prisoners, if they could get out of the bamboo houses, to cross the palisade and escape without attracting any notice. Two years ago it was the custom to keep a certain number of prisoners undergoing sentences of as much as six months at the lock–ups for the local labour.[3] At the Mathabhanga lock-up, one of the doors, which were made of wooden bars on a wooden framework, fastened with one padlock and chain half way from the ground to the top of the door, had got some what warped, and the prisoners found that they could prize it open at the bottom, without breaking the chain, sufficiently to admit of a man forcing his way through.[4] This was actually done for a short time, systematically and on dark and rainy nights certain prisoners used to get out of the lockup, go and commit thefts in the neighbourhood, dispose of their booty to accomplices outside and then return and lock themselves out.

Theft was reported to which no clue could be obtained, and the real delinquents might have escaped detection and served out their time in jail, committing thefts by night with impunity, had it not been for the discovery of some tobacco in the lock-up in possession of a prisoner, who when about to be punished, informed against his comrades rather than suffer alone and so the whole thing came out. The prisoners who had broken out confessed every thing. They had preferred returning to prison each night that they had got out, to remaining at large with warrants perpetually hanging over them.[5]

The story reflects small credit on any of the parties concerned but it was difficult to find fault, as the system was most to blame. One head constable and four constables were quite an inefficient guard for a lock-up and station house with a treasure chest in it, outside the lock-up in closure. The guard has been doubled, the doors of the buildings inside the lockup secured with double locks above and below and the sub-divisional officers prohibited from keeping prisoners sentenced to more than one weeks of rigorous imprisonment in the lock-up.[6]

Working of the Police force in the State :[7]

Details	*1877 -78*	*1878 -79*
Cognizable cases reported including those pending Police enquiry	1,586	1,577
A Forms (true)	371	368
A Forms (false)	0	1
B Forms (true)	23	35
B Forms (false)	10	5
C Forms (True)	320	387
C Forms (false)	154	200
Cases not enquired into under sec.117 code of pending Police enquiry	278	169
Cases taken up direct by Magistrate	362	396
Pending before the police at the close of the year	68	16

It will be observed that the number of A forms has decreased by 3. There is a decrease of 9 in the number of cases reported. The number of false cases, 206 against 164 of the previous year, shows an increase of 42 cases. Besides the false cases mentioned above, 82 cases were found to be false amongst those that were taken up direct by the Magistrates. The total number of false cases was therefore 288, or 20 percent of the total number of cognizable cases reported. 30 complainants were prosecuted under sections 182 and 211 for lodging false complaints, of whom 19 were convicted and 11 released.[8] Such an issue may be consider eminently satisfactory, knowing the difficulty of obtaining legal proof of the fact that a charge is false, however morally convinced as to its falsity one may be. Cases moreover are shown as false in the statements which are thrown out as being properly cognizable by the Civil courts, although the charges made may have their foundations in fact and such cases go to diminish the proportion of convictions under sections 182 and 211, to the total number of charges shown as false in the statements.[9]

During the year under report one sub –inspector, five head constables and 25 constables were punished for various offences under the Penal code. There was no cases of extortion of confession by torture, or cruelty against any of the police. The Fouzdari Ahilkar however notices that cases of oppression by chowkidars have come to his notice, in which he has little doubt that the chowkidars were only the tools of the regular police.Exemplary punishment has been dealt out in each cases and when the chowkidars come to understand their position better and learn their duties considered complaints will be of rare occurrence. They arise out of an exaggerated idea entertained by the chowkidar of the power of the regular policeman over him personally.[10] Out of the 930 taluk in the State 829 have 1,534 chowkidars and 101 still remain without chowkidars. Petitions for the appointment of chowkidars were came in. Hitherto the State has spent nothing on this new auxiliary Police force. It will be advisable also I think to adopt the rules in force in the neighbouring districts of Rungpore and Jalpaiguri regarding chowkidars for the better control of this large body of men.[11]

As before stated these chowkidars are paid by voluntary contributions. With a view to enforcing the continuance of such payments, without at the same time alarming the people with the idea of a new tax called for a report as to the distribution and incidence of the gross payments, preparatory to recommending that rules be passed to enable to realize from defaulters their quota of subscription and to fix the proportions in which the different grades of tenants shall pay according to the size of their holdings, &c. in the future.[12]

The following two tables shows the percentage of acquittals to convictions in cognizable cases taken up direct by Magistrates and in cases sent up by the police separately:[13]

Total number of persons in columns XV of cognizable return	*Acquitted &c. Columns XVI and XVII*	*Convicted &c., Columns XVIII A and B*	*Pending &c., Columns XIX, XXII, XIII*	*Percentage of conviction*
912	296	601	15	67

Results of trial persons in cognizable cases investigated by Police

Persons sent up for trial including those pending from last year	*Acquitted &c.*	*Convicted*	*Pending and died*	*Percentage of conviction*
578	138	428	12	75.6

The following officers are mentioned as specially deserving of commendable for detective ability:[14]

Sub Inspector Guru Prosanno Singh

Sub Inspector Mamtazuddin

Sub Inspector Mohamed Johar

Head Constable Nozeeruddin.

Inspector Parbutty Charan Chucerbutty also deserves favourable mention as an officer of intelligence and ability. In 1880–81 the statement regarding the Working of the Police force in the State were as follows :[15]

Details	*1879-80*	*1880-81*
Cognizable cases reported including those	1,255	1,048

conviction		
A Forms (true)	258	234
B Forms (true)	18	12
B Forms (false)	8	9
C Forms (True)	312	224
C Forms (false)	127	89
Cases not enquired into under sec.117 code of conviction	194	169
Cases taken up direct by Magistrate	326	302
Pending enquiry at the close of the year	12	9
Total	1,255	1,048

The number of A Forms is 234 against 258 of the preceding year, showing a decrease of 24; but considering that the total number of cases instituted directly before the Police was 746 against 929 or 183 cases less than those in the previous year. The number of false cases has also come down from 135 to 98 only. Eleven men were prosecuted for institution false cases; of those nine were convicted and two released. These prosecutions, probably had much to do with the reduction of false complaints.[16]

The following table shows the result of trial of persons in cognizable cases investigated by the State Police as compared with those of the previous year :[17]

Year	*Persons sent up for trial including those from last year*	*Acquitted*	*Convicted*	*Pending, died &c.*	*Percentage of convictions*
1879 – 80	434	95	311	28	76.6
1880 – 81	432	106	310	16	74.5

Regarding the number of village chowkidars, at the end of the year was 1554. Applications were received from the residents of five taluks during the year, five men were appointed with the sanction of the authorities. The total number of chowkidars in the Raj was 1,559. During the year a proposal for the introduction of the Government Chowkidari Act into this Raj is under consideration. The general conduct of the force has been good. The Superintendent of Police was not in charge during the entire year. During his absence Babu Sitanath Banerjee was incharge of the police office. On return of Babu Jadab Chander Chackerbutty, Fouzdari Ahilkar, Babu Satya Chanran Mukherjee reverted to his own appointment on 16th September 1880. Under the orders of the Governmnet contained in letter No.377 of 23rd February 1881, Mr. H.N.Harris, District Superintendent of Police of Rungpore, was specially deputed to inspect and report upon the working of the police in Cooch Behar. This officer visited all the police stations and made a careful inspection of the office of the Superintendent and submitted an exhaustive report in which he made a great many suggestions for the general improvement of the Police in the State. The chief points noted by him were as follows :[18]

- That some special rules should be drawn up for keeping all books, registers, files &c., especially the Registers of convicts (which is complete) and absconded prisoners. That the mode of keeping accounts, cash, &c. are faulty and should be remodeled in the Bengal system.
- That new accoutrements are required of the Regulation pattern.
- That the Inspectors and Sub –Inspectors are as intelligent a body as ant in Bengal and the men appeared to be a fine well set up lot of up country men and that local recruiting should be encouraged as much as possible.
- That a Sub Inspector on Rs. 60 should not be wasted upon drilling duty only. A man on Rs. 25 could be found perfectly competent for his duty.
- That promotion has been fairly and equally distributed.
- That there should be a half yearly inspection by the Superintendent of all the offices, Police stations and out-posts under his charge and that the results of this inspection should be recorded in writing

with the remarks of the inspecting officer.

- That instead of three Inspectors one would be sufficient for Cooch Behar.
- That the proportion of cases not enquired into under Section 117 of the Procedure Code is too high
- That there is very great delay in the submission of special reports from the office of the Superintendent of Police.
- That although cases are taken up very promptly at the Police stations, the diaries are not sufficiently concise.
- That the superintendent bore a very high character in the Rajshye and Pubna Police and that he has taken great pains with the Cooch Behar Force and that he is an intelligent and hard working officer but that a little more personal supervision over the conduct of enquires into cases should be exercised by him.

With regard to the Mr. Harris remarks that the Superintendent should exercise a little more personal supervision over the enquiry into cases.

In 1883 – 84 The Superintendent makes the following remark regarding the chowkidary system :[19]

> "This institution is as it were, 'back bone of a country' and wherever measures have been adopted for bettering the position of the Chowkidars by ensuing regularity of payment of their wages, they have worked well and acted as a medium between the villagers and the Police in the way of rendering assistance in the investigation of cases. The want of an Act to ensure regularity of payment of their wages is greatly felt and the sooner Act VI of 1870 with modifications adopted to this country is introduced here, the better will they do their

work."

During the year trial of persons in cognizable cases investigated by State Police :[20]

Year	*Persons sent up for trial including those from last year*	*Acquitted*	*Convicted*	*Pending, died &c.*	*Percentage of convictions*
1882 – 83	494	123	337	34	73.26
1883 – 84	444	108	296	40	73.26

Regarding the Dak establishment it can be noted that the establishment worked well during the year under report. Two more runners were appointed on the removal of the Tufangunj station to Fulbari and Bhoishkuchi out-post to Modhurbasha.[21]

In 1890 there were a number of municipal police was appointed in the State. The chowkidars watch over the town and the jamadar goes on round duty, posts of chowkidars to their respective beats and supervises their work. Sub inspector exercise a general control over this force. The total amount cost of the Force was Rs. 2,211 – 6 including the price of clothing supplied to them from the State on the occasion of the visit of their Excellencies the Viceroy and Governor General of India and Lady Lansdown to Cooch Behar.[22]

In 1890 the work of reform was going on in Bengal for the better administration of police work. As the Cooch Behar State Police is organized on the model of the Bengal Police, that the suggestions made by the police commission and acted up to by the Bengal Government may as far as possible be followed for the efficient administration of the Police. The subject has been put in front of the Maharaja in Council and it has been decided to allow certain concessions as regards pay and clothing allowance to the men subjected to the superannuation fund rules which have been given effect to from the beginning of the current year.[23]

The Cooch Behar State military force was at the peak

point during the rule of the Maharaja Nripendra Narayan. The Subadar Major, Momin Khan, has been distinctly given to understand that unless he can enforce greater efficiency and ensure the maintenance of stricter discipline among the men, the question of the retention of his service will have to be considered. The conduct of jamadar was also under the supervision of the Major. [24]

In 1895 The State Police Force was in charge of the Cooch Behar State Railway Police which consists of one head constable and two constables, were sent by the Assistant Inspector General of Railway police to take charge of the line and they were posted by the above offers as follows :[25]

One constable at Gitaldaha, one constable at Dewanhat and one Head Constable at Chowrahat. The Superintendent of Police is of opinion that the men should be posted as follows:

1 Constable at Gitaldaha, 1 constable at Chowrahat, 1 Head–Constable at Torsha.

In 1897–98 the Superintendant of the State said that "The Chowkidars have on the whole done good work during the year, for which they have been rewarded. The system of rewarding the Chowkidars in case of good attendance and punishing them otherwise which had introduced about 3 years ago has had a great effect in improving their attendance and consequently the Police receive reports regularly of crime &c., now a days."

From the above analysis it can be said that a systematic system of law and order has been maintained by the Cooch Behar State during the rule of Maharaja Nripendra Narayan, which set an example of modern means of administrative measures from the royal authority.

NOTES AND REFERENCES

1. Annual Administration Report of the Cooch Behar State (1878 - 79), p.38.
2. *Ibid*.
3. *Ibid*.

4. *Ibid*.
5. *Ibid*.
6. *Ibid*., p. 39.
7. *Ibid*.
8. *Ibid*.
9. *Ibid*., p. 40.
10. *Ibid*.
11. *Ibid*., p. 41.
12. *Ibid*.
13. *Ibid*.
14. *Ibid*., p. 42.
15. Annual Administration Report of the Cooch Behar State (1880-81), p. 36.
16. *Ibid*.
17. *Ibid*., p. 37.
18. *Ibid*., p. 38.
19. Annual Administration Report of the Cooch Behar State (1883 – 84), p. 17.
20. *Ibid*., p. 18.
21. *Ibid*., p. 19.
22. Annual Administration Report of the Cooch Behar State (1891 – 92), p. 18.
23. *Ibid*.
24. Annual Administration Report of the Cooch Behar State (1893 – 94), p. 65.
25. Annual Administration Report of the Cooch Behar State (1895 – 96), p. 32.
26. Annual Administration Report of the Cooch Behar State (1897 – 98), p. 16.

4

Conclusion

The history of the princely State of Cooch Behar entered into a new paradigm with the accession of Maharaja Nripendra Narayan, although he was placed at a minor age with the support of the Principal officers of the State along with the Maharanis namely Kameswari, Vrindeswari and Nistarini Devi in 1863. The succession was subsequently confirmed by the British Government in January 1864. A will was set up on behalf of the three Maharanis, appointing them joint Sarvarahakars during the minority of Nripendra Narayan. On enquiry it was set aside by Government as not genuine.[1] In consequence of dissensions in the family and the fear that evil result would arise there form, the Government resolved upon assuming charge of the State during the minority of its chief and deputed Colonel J.C. Haughton, Governor– General's Agent, North–East Frontier, to Cooch Behar as Commissioner in charge of the administration. Such a step was considered by Government to be imperatively called for as the only means of effectually providing for the care and education of the young Maharaja for the security of the tribute and for the defense of the Bhutan frontier, for the which the Government was responsible.[2] The Commissioner of Cooch Behar was vested by the Colonial Government with the full authority of the ruler of the State, except in regard to certain specified points, such as the grant of lands, of pensions and gratuities and the conformation of capital sentence. These duties of his office he was to exercise in direct communication with Government and not subject to the control of the Governor-general's Agent for the North- East Frontier.[3]

Colonel Haughton joined his duties as Commissioner in 1864 and except for an absence of a year and a half continued in his post still 1873. Besides the work of administration, an important part of his duty was to see that the young price was properly cared for and brought up, and this he appears to have done with almost paternal care and affection for his young ward. The value of the work done by that great administrator cannot be better expressed than in the following eloquent words of Mr. Dalton, Deputy Commissioner :[4]

" And up to the time of Sir George Campbell, writes Mr. Dalton, "Colonel Haughton appears to have always exercised the full powers thus confided to him and to have done so with a judgment and ability which combined with the personal interest which he displayed in all, even the most trivial matters connected with the administration, fully justified the confidence reposed in him and inaugurated that system of judicial and political reform and financial development which in the hands of his successors have made Cooch Behar what it is."

Colonel Haughton was succeeded as Commissioner by Colonel Bruce in June 1865, who again was relieved by Colonel Agnew; the latter officiated until Colonel Haughton's return in December 1866. Colonel Haughton continued to be at Cooch Behar until February 1873, when he finally left the State.[5] Mr. Richardson and Mr. Metcalf then in turn officiated as Commissioner up to the 1st March 1874, when Sir W.J. Herschel was appointed. Sir William Herschel left in 1875, when Mr.F.R. Cockerell became Commissioner for a year. He was the first Commissioner of the Rajshahi and Cooch Behar Division, the previous Commissioners having had the charge of the Cooch Behar Division only. Lord H. Ulick Browne succeeded Mr. Cockrell in 1876 and continued to be at the head of the Cooch Behar administration till the Maharaja attained his majority in October 1883 and received charge of his State from the Government.[6]

Colonel Haughton commenced as Commissioner of the Cooch Behar State only, on a salary of Rs. 2,000. When the Second Bhutan War broke out, a deputy Commissioner was appointed to assist Colonel Haughton, whose time was now entirely taken up with attending to political duties and transport matters connected with the expedition. After the conclusion of this war the Cooch Behar Division was formed comprising the districts of Darjeeling, Jalpaiguri, and Goalpara and the State of Cooch Behar to which Garo Hills was also added and Colonel Haughton was placed in charge of the Division. Jalpaiguri was then made the head quarters of the Commissioner and a large portion of the duties hitherto performed by him was delegated to the Deputy Commissioner who was the principal resident officer at Cooch Behar.[7]

The First Deputy Commissioner of Cooch Behar was Mr. H.Beveridge, cs., who took charge on the 4th November 1864.nHe was succeeded by Mr. T.Smith on the 1st May 1866 and made over charge to captain W. Lance in 1868. Captain Lance was relieved By Mr. W.O.A. Beckett on the 22nd December 1870, who in his turn was succeeded by Mr. Smith, who returned to Cooch Behar in February 1872, and remained till April 1875, when Captain Lewin relieved him.[8] Captain Lewin went on 6months leave in April 1876, and Mr. J.G.B.T.Dalton was appointed to officiate and subsequently confirmed, in the post at which he remained till the end of the British administration of the country with the exception of 3 months when he went on privilege leave, and Mr. E.A.Bradbury, c.s., officiated and again when on his taking furlough in 1881, Captain (afterwards Lieutenant–Colonel) A. Evens Gordon officiated till his return in December 1882.[9]

When Colonel Haughton assumed charge in 1864 Babu kamal Sanyal was the Dewan. That officer died in December 1868, when there was a short interregnum, during which the work was done by local officers. Rao Calica Das Dutt

Bahadur, B.L., afterwards created a Companion of the Indian Empire, the Head of the Revenue Administration and Senior Member of the State Council, who was then a Deputy Magistrate and Deputy Collector, was selected and appointed Dewan in August 1869 assumed charge of his office on the 23rd September of the year and was duly installed in a formal Darbar of usual state on the 12th February 1870.[10]

The Dewan was the head of the Revenue Department, the Dewani Ahilkar of civil and the Fouzdari Ahilkar of Criminal Justice. The Accounts, the Military and the Police as well as Education and Public Works were directly under the Deputy Commissioner, who was also the Session Judge and the Second Court of Appeal in Civil and criminal cases. The collection of land Revenue was made by the sub- divisional Naib Ahilkars under the supervision of the Dewan, who directly held charge of the Treasury. All the departments were placed under the Deputy Commissioner, the heist authority in all matters connected with the State resting with the commissioner, who exercised his powers subject to the control of the Supreme Government.[11]

The installation took place on the 8th November 1883, when the charge of the administration was formally made over to His Highness by His Honor the Lieutenant – Governor of Bengal. His Highness thought it advisable not to make any violent disturbances in the administrative arrangements, introduced after much consideration by the successive British Administrators. There was no interference with the continuity of the departmental work, although the division of authority and system of control underwent considerable changes.[12]

Under the Memorandum of Administration framed by the Commissioner of the Rajshahi and Cooch Behar Division and adopted by His Highness on the day following the Installation, a Council of State was established with His Highness as President and three members, namely the Superintendent of the State, the Dewan and a Judicial officer, who were to be the Heads of the three Departments of General administration, the administration of Revenue and that of Civil Justice.[13]

"In our absence", to quote from the proclamation issued by the his Highness on the day following the Installation "the Superintendant intended will act as vice-President of the Council.[14]

"The Superintendant will supervise, direct and control the administration of Criminal Justice and the Police, the military, public works, Education and Audit Departments and will be the Session judge, hearing all criminal appeals which ordinarily lie to the Session Judges, but will not act as a Civil Judge except when sitting in Council."[15]

The Dewan will be in charge of the Revenue Department being responsible for the collection of all kinds of Revenue and the supervision of all proceedings in connection therewith.[16]

The Judicial member of the Council will hear Civil and Revenue appeals of certain classes and supervise the administration of Civil Justice, all final appeals lying to the Council.

In December 1891, the Memorandum of Administration of 1883 was considerably modified. The constitution of the Council on the Judicial side was remodeled and a Court consisting of two members (the member from whom appeals lay before the Council being left out) similar to a Division Branch of the Calcutta High Court, was established. Any difference of opinion either upon evidence or upon a point of law between the two members was to be referred to a Full Bench consisting of all the members with the Maharaja as President. All motions against the orders of subordinate officers were to be heard by a Bench composed of all the three members of the Council.[17]

On the Legislative side, it was the intention of his Highness to appoint Additional members from time to time, from amongst the Rajguns, the intelligent and wealthy Jotedars and from the Bar.[18]

The power exercised by the Council and by the Heads of Departments as well as by the Manager for the chaklajat estate in sanctioning expenditure within their Budget allotments and in transferring savings from one head of the Budget to another were modified and curtailed.[19]

Provision was also made for the inspection of the offices of the Departmental Heads by the His highness and of the subordinate offices under the three departments, by the heads of the Departments.[20]

The Civil Judge was appointed Session Judge in addition to his duties and the Superintendent of the State ceased to be a Session Judge and the Dewan an Additional Sessions Judge to which office he had been appointed in 1890 – 91.[21]

The power of the Fouzdari Ahilkar were defined and made to correspond with those of a District Magistrates of British India. In this connection the powers of the superintendent of Police were also formally laid down.[22]

The Superintendent of works formerly enjoyed large powers. These were curtailed. The status of that officer was defined to be that of an Executive Engineer of Bengal, with certain modifications of the powers of sanctioning expenditure for original works and repairs and of appointment of subordinate officers and granting leave to them.[23]

From the above analysis it can be said that a well framed administrative structure has been maintained under the guidance of the Maharaja along with the help of the Colonial persons, and more specifically can be conclude that the period of modernization can easily be seen in each and every sphere of the State which was a unique feature of disciplinary work of the authority.

NOTES AND REFERENCES

1. Chowdhuri, H.N., *The Cooch Behar State and its Land Revenue Settlement*, Cooch Behar state Press, Cooch Behar, 1903, p. 287.
2. *Ibid*.
3. *Ibid*.
4. *Ibid*.

5. *Ibid.*
6. *Ibid.*, p. 288.
7. *Ibid.*
8. *Loc.cit.*
9. *Ibid.*, p. 289.
10. *Ibid.*
11. *Ibid.*
12. *Ibid.*
13. *Ibid.*
14. *Ibid.*
15. *Ibid.*, p. 290.

The Memorandum of administration is quoted below in extensor:

- The Maharaja is satisfied that the present system of administration under which the State and its people have prospered and made such satisfactory progress, and for which he is much indebted to the British Government, leaves nothing to be desired and that if he was in a position to assume the functions and duties of supervision now discharged by the Commissioner and in some cases by Government, no change whatever would be necessary. The Maharaja feels, however, that his youth and inexperience in Executive and Judicial business would place him at a disadvantage if he acted alone, and therefore while reserving to himself the right to exercise hereafter all the authority and powers wielded by his predecessors should he think fit to do so, he has resolved to act for the present in some important matters by and with the advice of a Council. The following is a general sketch of the system he intends to adopt and he trusts that he may have the approval of the British Government in regard to it:
- The Cooch Behar State Council will consist of three Members with the Maharaja as President. The members will be the Superintendent of the State, Dewan, and an experienced Judicial officer whose services the Maharaja hopes to obtain from the British Government. In the Maharaja's absence the Superintendent will act as vice- President of the Council. Three members will be entirely independent of each other, and it will be the duty of each to see that all measures &c., decided on in council are carried out, he reporting at the next meeting what has been done in the mater.
- The annual state budget will, after the officers in charge of the Departments have submitted their proposals and after those proposals have been considered by the members of the Council, be brought up

and discussed in Council, after which it will be submitted to the Maharaja for sanction, without which the budget will not be finally settled. Expenditure in excess of the Budget will not be incurred under any hearing without the Mahäraja's sanction. When he has sanctioned the budget, it will rest, as at present, with the Heads of the Departments to spend within certain limits their allotments in accordance with the details of the budget and it will be duty of the State auditor to check the expenditure. Each member of the Council will be at liberty to transfer savings under one head of the budget to another under which additional expenditure is thought necessary or advisable, provide that both heads come under the member's department. In cases in which the sanction of the Deputy Commissioner is now required it will be accorded by the three members of the Council, each for his own Department and in cases where the Commissioner's sanction is now sanction of the Council will be necessary. The disposal of all surpluses revenue in excess of the budget will rest entirely with the Maharaja.

- The Superintendent of the State will supervise, direct and control the administration of criminal Justice and the police, military, jail, public works, Education and Audit Departments and will be Session Judge hearing al criminal appeals which ordinarily lie to Session Judges but will not act as a Civil Judge except when sitting in Council.
- The Dewan will be in charge of the Revenue Department, being responsible for the collection of all kinds of revenue and the supervision of all proceedings in connection therewith. The treasury officer will be his subordinate and it will be the Dewan's duty to test the cash, notes and stamp balances once in every three months on fixed dates. The Dewan will not exercise Judicial powers appeals from the decisions of his subordinates in rent suits lying to the Civil Court, but he will hear appeals from their orders in revenue executive matters, such as sales for arrears, mutation cases &c.
- The Judicial Member of Council will hear all Civil and Revenue appeals, in which the subject matter of the suit exceeds in value Rs. 100 in Small Cause Court Cases and Rs. 50 in other cases and he will in addition try original Civil and Rent suits in which the value exceeds Rs. 500. This distribution of Judicial business istentative only, and will be liable to modification.
- The following appeals will lie to the Council :
    - i) Appeals from sentences passed by Session Court.
    - ii) Civil appeals, both on the facts and on points of law from the decision of the Judicial Member in original suits and
    - iii) Special appeal on law points only in other Civil and Revenue cases, Sentences of death must be confirmed by the Council

in every case and no appeals will be necessary.

- The Assistant Ahilkar of the Malcutchery or Revenue Department will be in charge of the Treasury and in all matters not otherwise provided form this memorandum. The Head of the departments will exercise the powers and discharge duties now constructed to them.
- No new tax will be imposed by the Maharaja without the consent of his Council, but it will be open to him to veto any such tax proposed by the Council. No salaries will be altered, and no establishment changed either by reductions or additional appointments, except by the decision of the Council confirmed by the Maharaja. It will be the duty of the Council to consult the Maharaja in all matters of importance, and by letter if necessary. If he disapproves of any measure passed in his absence, he will call a full meetings of the council, at which he will himself preside, and to reopen the question. The Maharaja will have two votes when presiding in the Council and each of the member one vote. Matters specially reserved for the Maharaja's decision or authority will not be settled in Council at all, though the Maharaja may consult any members of it as he pleases. Questions coming before the council will be decides by a majority of votes.
- As regards the Chaklajat estates in British territory, the Budget will be prepared by the Manager and settled in Council after which the Manager will be allowed to spend money within budget limits under each heading within the following limits. For expenditure will require no sanction as regards matters sanctioned by the District officer in the case of Wards Estates of British territory. In matters requiring in British Districts the sanction of the Commissioner, the sanction of the Council must be obtained. The Manager will be allowed to transfer savings under one head of the budget to another head.

  He will institute rent suits and institute and defend ordinary civil suits without sanction, taking legal advice on the principles adopted in estates under the Court of Wards. Important matters, which thought not involving expenditure would by their nature be submitted to the Commissioner if the Estates were still under the Court of Wards, will be laid before the Council and the same as regards the institution or defense of Civil suits of great importance or involving large amounts. The business connected with the Chaklajat Estates to be settled in Council, will ordinarily be taken up once or twice a month and for such matters (only) the Manager will be a member of Council with a vote like the other members. In the vent of the votes of the Council being equally divided, the Vice President will, in the Maharaja's absence, have a casting vote. It will be the duty of the Council to consult the Maharaja in matters of special importance connected with these estates, and he will re-open matters, as provided in para 9 of this memorandum, if he disapproves of the decisions or orders of the

Council issued in his absence.

K) Neither the Council nor the Administration of Cooch Behar will with the exception of the Audit Department, have anything to do with the Maharaja's Estate in Darjeeling. All the business connected with this property will be carried on by the Agent in direct communication with the Maharaja, the state Auditor continuing to audit the expenditure as at present. Any difference of opinion between Agent and the Auditor will be referred for the decision of the Maharaja.

16. *Ibid*.,p291.
17. *Ibid*.,p,292.
18. *Ibid*.
19. *Ibid*.
20. *Ibid*., p. 293.
21. *Ibid*., p. 294.
22. *Ibid*., p. 295.
23. *Ibid*.

Bibliography

Primary Source:

a) Manuscript

1) Home Public Proceedings (Relevant Volumes).

2) Board of Revenue Proceedings (Relevant Volumes).

3) Proceedings of the Governor General – in – Council (Relevant Volumes).

b) Official Documents

Annual Administration Report of the Cooch Behar State (1862 –1950).

Cooch Behar Census Report – 1951, 1961.

Cooch Behar Darpan – 14th April, 1938.

The Cooch Behar Gazette – (1896, 1910, 1914, 1923, 1926, 1932, 1934, 1937, 1938, 1945, 1947).

Cooch Behar Select Records, vol. – I & II, Cooch Behar State Press, 1884.

Hunter, W.W – *A Statistical Account of Bengal,* vol. X, 6 th ed., London.

Jenkins, F. – *Papers on Cooch Behar, Selection from Bengal Government,* No. 5, Calcutta –1851.

Majumdar, Durgadas – *West Bengal District Gazetteers* (Koch Bihar), Feb., 1977.

C) Memoirs

1) Chawdhuri, Deendoyal, *Nripendra Smiriti,* Calcutta, 1915.
2) Devi, Gayatri and Ram, Santha, *The Memoirs of the Maharani of Jaipur, A Princess Remembers,* Vikas Publishing house Pvt. Ltd, New Delhi, 1982.
3) Das, Biswanath (ed.), *Autobiography of an Indian Princess – Memoirs of Maharani Sunity Devi of Cooch Behar,* Vikash Publishing House Pvt. Ltd., New Delhi, 1995.
4) Narayan, Nripendra, *Thirty Seven Years of Big game Shooting, Cooch Behar (The Duars & Assam),* Bombay, The Times Press, 1908.

Secondary Source :

a) Books (English)

Barma, Sukhbilas (ed.), *Socio-Political Movements in North Bengal: A Sub – Himalayan Tract, Vol. I & II,* Global Vision Publishing House, Delhi, 2007.

Barman, Rupkumar, *From Tribalism To State,* Abhijeet Publications, Delhi, 2007.

Bhattachariya, P.K., *The Kingdom of Kamta Koch Behar in Historical Perspective,* Ratna Publication & N.B.U., 2000.

Campbell, Arthur Claude, *Glimpses of Bengal, Vol –I,* 3 &4 Hare Street, Calcutta, 1907.

Chaudhuri, H.N., *The Cooch Behar State and its Land Revenue Settlement,*

Cooch Behar State Press, Cooch Behar, 1903.

Copland, Ian, *The British Raj and The Indian Princes Paramountcy in Western India (1857–1930)*, Orient Longman, Bombay, 1987.

Dasgupta, Ranajit, *Economy, Society and Politics in Bengal : Jalpaiguri, (1869–1947)*, Oxford University Prees, Bombay, 1992.

Deb, Ranajit, *North Bengal at a Glance - Cooch Behar, Jalpaiguri, Darjeeling, Vol. I*, Purbouttar Prakashan, Kolkata, 2002.

Debnath, Sailen (ed.), *Social And Political Tensions In North Bengal (Since – 1947)*, N.L. Publishers, Siliguri, 2007.

Debnath, Sailen, *Essays on Cultural History of North Bengal*, N.L. Publishers, Siliguri, 2008.

Fisher, Michael H., *Indirect Rule in India – Residents and the Residency System (1764 - 1858)*, Oxford University Press, 1991.

Gait, Edward, *A History of Assam*, Surjeet Publications, 4 th Reprint, Delhi, 2008.

Ganguli, Karali Charan, *Final Report on the Survey and Settlement Operations in the Cooch Behar State*, (1913 – 1927), Cooch Behar State Press, Cooch Behar, 1930.

Ghoshal, S.C., *A History of Cooch Behar* (Translation), Cooch Behar State Press, Cooch Behar, 1942.

Hunter, W.W., *The Annals of Rural Bengal*, London, 1897.

Jehangir, Sarabji, *Princes and Chiefs of India, Vol. II*, London, 1903.

Kerr, Ian. J, *Building the Railway of the Raj (1850 – 1900)*, Oxford University Press, Delhi, 1997.

Majumdar, Prof. Amlanjyoti, *Literary Works of Maharaja Jitendra Narayan Bhup Bahadur of Cooch Behar,* N.L. Publisher, Siliguri, 2010.

Majumdar, R.C, *History of Modern Bengal, Part one (1765-1905)*, G. Bharadwaj & Co., Calcutta, 1978.

Mukherjee, B.N. (ed.), *Early Historical Perspective of North Bengal*, N.B.U., 1987.

Nag, Hiten (ed.), *Cooch Beharer Itihas*, N.L.Publisher, Siliguri, 2005.

Nag, Hiten (ed.), *America through Hindu Eyes*, N.L.Publisher, Siliguri, 2004.

Pal, Joydeep, *The Untold History of the Princely State of Cooch Behar*, Sopan Publisher, Kolkata, 2015.

Pal, Joydeep, *The multi avenues of revenue management and settlement operation system in Cooch Behar – A study of the monarchical achievement*, Sopan publisher, Kolkata, 2015.

Pal, Joydeep, *The Cooch Behar State and its History of Modernity (1839-1950)*, Abhijeet Publications, New Delhi, 2017.

Pal, Joydeep, *Glimpses of Cooch Behar State : A model State in Colonial Writings*, Abhijeet Publications, New Delhi, 2019.

Rhodes, Nicholas & Bose, Shankar .K., *The Coinage of Cooch Behar*, Library of Numismatic Studies, Dhubri, India, 1999.

Sanyal, Charu Chandra, *Rajbansis of North Bengal, Vol. xi*, Asiatic Society, Calcutta, 1965.

Sanyal, Ratna Roy, *The Raj and the Princely State of Cooch Behar – A* Study of Anglo–Cooch Behar Relations (1772– 1839), Dipali Publishers, Chanchal, Malda, 2004.

Sarkar, Anil Kumar, *British Paramountcy and the Cooch Behar State*, Abhijeet Publications, Delhi, 2011.

Sarkar, Ichhimuddin, *Aspects of Historical Geography of Pragjyotisa – Kamarupa (Ancient Assam)*, Naya Prokash, Calcutta, 1992.

Books (Bengali)

Achrya, Sujit Kumar, *Kam Kamta Kamakhya Tatha koch Rajbansider Dravidio Utshya*, Indiana, Kolkata, 2007.

Ahmed, Amanutullah, *History of Cooch Behar* (in Bengali), Cooch Behar State Press, 1936.

Bandhopadhaya, Amiya Kumar & Das, Sudhir Ranjan (ed.), *Cooch Behar Zillar Purakirti*, Puratattya Bibhag, Government of West Bengal, 1974 .

Bandhopadhaya, Tapas Kumar, *Koch O Totoder Samaj Sanskriti*, Pratibhas, Kolkata, 2008.

Bandapadhaya, Bhagavatee Charan, *Cooch Beharer Itihas*, Cooch Behar State Press, Cooch Behar, 1882.

Barma, Hemanta Kumar Roy, *Cooch Beharer Itihas*, Pranati Books, Cooch Behar, Reprint, 2005.

Bhattachariya, Gauri Sankar, *Uttarbanger Pathe Pathe*, Economic Book Stall, Siliguri, 2005.

Bhattacharya, Himadri Sankar, *Cooch Behar O Prachin Prathar Kichu Jana O Ajana Katha*, Madhurima Ofset, Cooch Behar, 2002.

Dalai, Ghanashyam, *Sachitra Kuchbehar - Rajchitra*, Kuntalin Press, Calcutta, 1915.

Das, Bhagirath (ed.), *Cooch Behar Loksanskrit Utsav - Smarak Grantha* Floriculturist Research Institute of Cooch Behar, Cooch Behar, 2001.

Das, Biswanath, *Maharanee Sunity Devi - Coochbehar Maharanee Sunity Devir Jiban Katha* (in Bengali), Sishu Sahitya Sansad, Calcutta, 2000.

Das, Biswanath (ed.), *Rajopakhyan*, Mala Publications, Calcutta, 1985.

Deb, Ranajit, *Cooch Beharer Itihas*, Delta Farma, Calcutta, 2005.

Deb, Ranajit, *Cooch Beharer Eitijhyamoyee Rajprasad*, Purbottar Prakashan, Calcutta, 1999.

Deb, Saswati, *Cooch Behar Parichaya*, Purbouttar Prakashan, Cooch Behar, 2006.

Debnath, Mahendra, *Shahar Cooch Beharer Tinsha Bachar*, Vikash Publishar, Kolkata, 2007.

Debnath, Mahendra, *Atmakathane Cooch Behar Maharani Brindeswari o Jenkins School*, Lekhapara Publisher, Cooch Behar, 2010.

Devi, Brindeswari, *Beharodanta*, Kakiniyastha Printer, Cooch Behar, 1859.

Dey, Dilip Kumar, *Cooch Beharer Lokosanskriti*, Anima Prakashani, Calcutta, 2007.

Ghosh, Ananda Gopal & Das, Nilangshu Sekhar, *Uttar Banger Itihas o Samaj*, Dipali Publisher, Malda, 2009.

Halder, Sashibhusan, *Cooch Behar Hitaishinee Sabha Baktritamala*, Cooch Behar, 1965.

Majumdar, Arun Bhusan, *Pratyush O Pradosh Kaler Kamta - Cooch Behar*, Arya Publishing House, New Delhi, 2008.

Majumdar, Shubhendu, *Adhunik Siksha O Cooch Behar Victoriya College (·– 1938)*, West Bengal state Book Board, 2000.

Pal, Joydeep, *Oitijhyabahi Cooch Beharer Itihaser Ruprekha*, Progressive Publisher, Kolkata, 2016.

Paul, Nripendra Nath, *Itikathay Cooch Behar*, Anima Prakashani, Kolkata, 2000.

Paul, Nripendra Nath (ed.), *Koch Kings Of Kamrup*, Anima Prakashani, Calcutta, 1985.

Paul, Nripendra Nath (ed.), *Maharaj Harendra Narayan O Shibendra Narayaner Bhaktigiti Sangraha*, Anima Prakashani, Kolkata, 1999.

Ray, Schindra Nath, *Sahitya Sadhanaya Rajanya Shasita Koch Behar*, Supreme Publishers, Kolkata, 1999.

Ray, Swapan Kumar, *Prachin Koch Beharer Sampurna Itibritta*, Baiwala, Kolkata, 2006.

Ray, Swapan Kumar, *Prachin Koch Beharer Aartho- Samajik Itihas*, Baiwala, Kolkata, 2008.

Ray, Swapan Kumar, *Kochbihar Rajdarabarer Sahityacharcha*, Books Way Publisher, Kolkata, 2011.

Roy, Abhijit, *Koch Behar Raj-Jnankosh (1510 –1949)*, Anima Prakashani, Kolkata, 2002 .

Sanyal, Soven, *Alipurduarer Pathe Prantare*, Alipurduar Nature Club, Alipurduar Court, 2006.

Sanyal, Soven, *Cooch Behar Kichu Katha, Kichu Itihas*, Alipurduar Nature Club, Alipurduar Court, 2008.

Sarker, Abhijit, *Cooch Beharer Chithi*, Cooch Behar Press, Cooch Behar, 2004.

b) Unpublished Ph.D Dissertations :

Das, Kamalesh Chandra, " Modernisation of a Princely State Cooch Behar under the Maharaja Nripendra Narayan (1863 – 1911)", Department of History, University of North Bengal.

Sen, Partha Kumar, " Study of some aspects of the history of Kamata Cooch Behar since 1772 to the date of Accession of Shivendra Narayan",

Department of History ,University of North Bengal.

Sircar, Sekhar, " Land Settlement and Revenue Administration and taxation under the Maharajas of Cooch Behar State, (1773 – 1949)", Department of Economics, University of North Bengal.

c) Journals, Magazines, News Paper

Achrya, Nirmalya (ed.), *Ekkhan*, 1995-96.

Bengal past & Present – 2002.

Bhattachariya, Ajitesh (ed.), *Madhuparni,* Vol. of Cooch Behar (ed.) by Ananda Gopal Ghosh, August, 1990.

Bhattachariya, Aninda & Biswas, Rajarshi (ed.), Manshai, (2007 & 2008).

Chaki, Debabrata (ed.), *Uttar Prasanga*, Vol. 1, 2, 3 (2008).

Das, Sukhendu (ed.)- Cooch Behar Zilla Sankha, Dept. of information & Culture, Govt. of West Bengal, July, 2006.

Smaranika (Dinhata Municipality), Cooch Behar, 4 th Oct., 2002.

Smaranika (Jenkins School), 2011.

Smaranika (Khudra Patra- Patrika Parishad, Uttar Banga, 17-19, Dec., 2010.

Smaranika (North Bengal State Library), Cooch Behar, 1996.

Smaranika (Sunity Academy), 1981, 2006.

Uttarbanga Sambad, 17 th, August, 2008.

Index